THE COMPLETE
CHILDREN'S
ATLAS

THE COMPLETE
CHILDREN'S
ATLAS

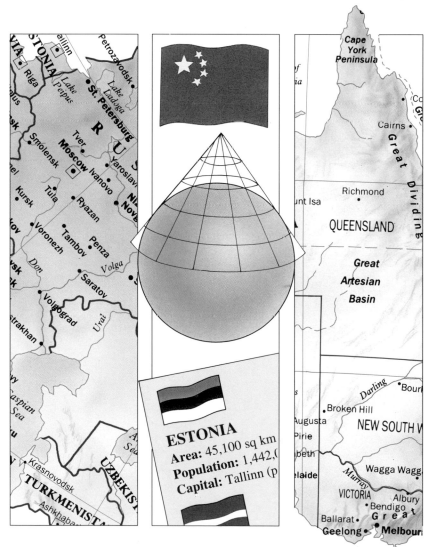

MALCOLM PORTER

CHERRYTREE BOOKS

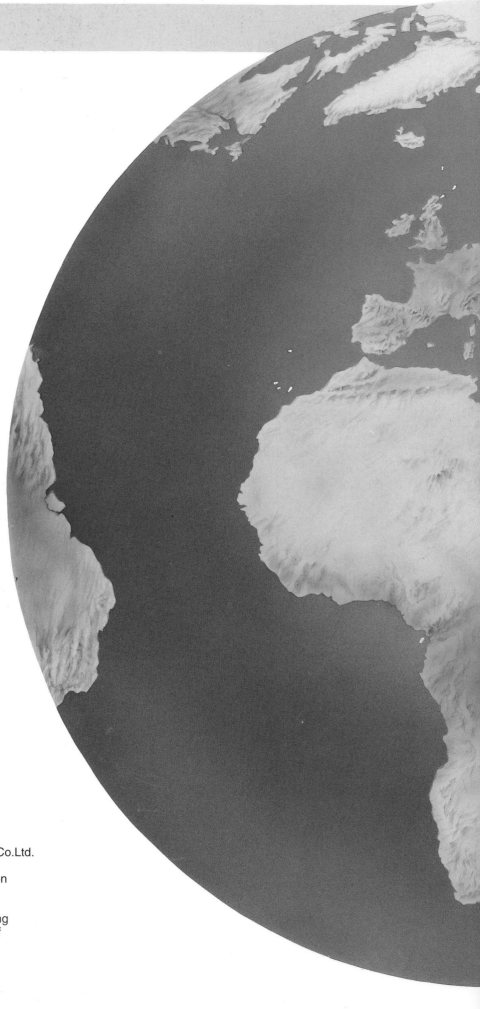

A Cherrytree Book

Designed and produced by
A S Publishing
Consultant editor Keith Lye
Assistant editor Paul Dempsey

This revised and updated edition first
published 2004
by Cherrytree Books, part of the
Evans Publishing Group
2A Portman Mansions
Chiltern St
London W1U 6NR

First published 1993
as The Cherrytree Children's Atlas

British Library Cataloguing in Publication
data
Porter, Malcolm
    The complete children's atlas
            1.Children's atlases 2.Atlases,
            British-Juvenile literature
            I.Title
            912
ISBN 184234207X
13 digit ISBN (from 1January 2007)
97818342342077

Printed in Hong Kong by New Era Printing Co.Ltd.

CONTENTS

Planet Earth

Our Earth is one of the nine planets that circle the Sun. It is the third planet from the Sun. Today, we can see photographs of the Earth taken from space. These show land areas, called continents, and blue seas and oceans.

Maps show the same things, but they give much more information than space photographs. They show the names and positions of cities and towns, and other features such as rivers and mountains.

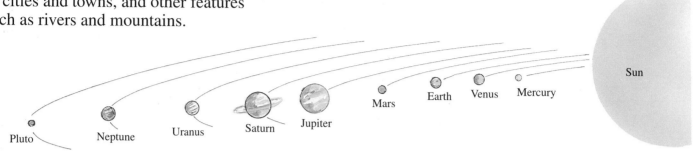

Pluto   Neptune   Uranus   Saturn   Jupiter   Mars   Earth   Venus   Mercury   Sun

As the Earth circles the Sun, it spins on its axis, an imaginary line joining the North Pole, the centre of the Earth and the South Pole.

Some lines appear on maps. One line around the middle of the Earth, exactly halfway between the North and South Poles, is called the Equator. Other lines are called the Tropic of Cancer in the northern half of the world, and the Tropic of Capricorn in the southern half. Two important lines go round the cold areas near the poles. They are the Arctic and Antarctic Circles.

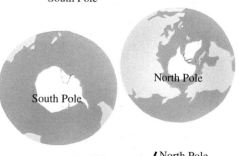

Land areas		
	Area (sq km)	Area (sq miles)	Population
North America	24,249,000	9,363,000	480,514,000
South America	17,835,000	6,886,000	340,536,000
Europe*	6,222,600	2,402,000	596,495,000
Russia	17,075,400	6,593,000	146,200,000
Asia*	31,181,000	12,039,000	3,585,512,000
Africa	30,330,000	11,694,000	779,181,000
Australia and the Pacific	8,508,000	3,285,000	30,196,000
Antarctica	14,000,000	5,400,000	

*Excluding Russia

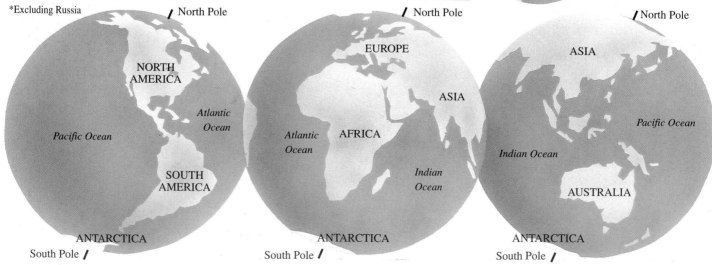

6

World records

Mountains
The highest mountains in five continents are shown on the right. The world's highest peak is Mount Everest.

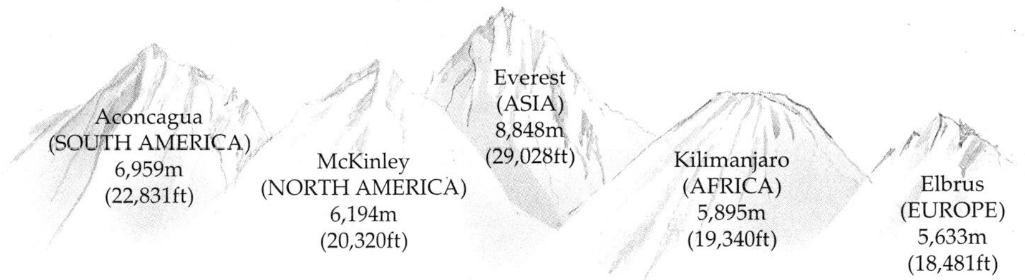

Aconcagua
(SOUTH AMERICA)
6,959m
(22,831ft)

McKinley
(NORTH AMERICA)
6,194m
(20,320ft)

Everest
(ASIA)
8,848m
(29,028ft)

Kilimanjaro
(AFRICA)
5,895m
(19,340ft)

Elbrus
(EUROPE)
5,633m
(18,481ft)

Rivers
The world's longest rivers are the Nile in Africa and the Amazon in South America.

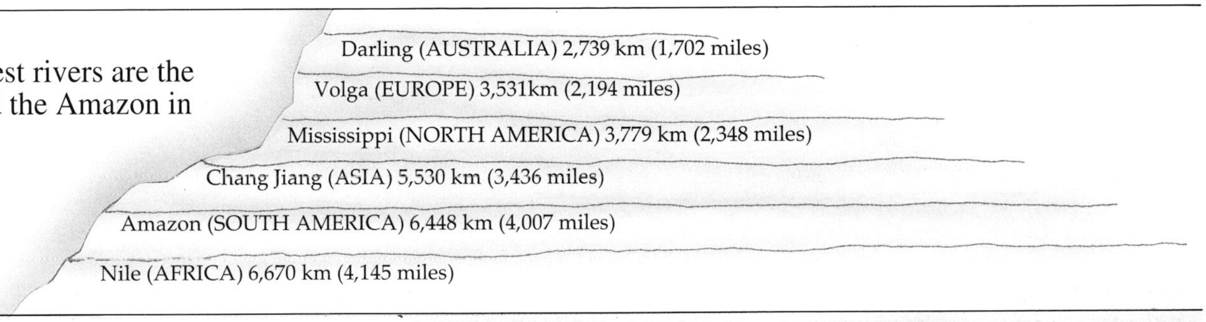

Darling (AUSTRALIA) 2,739 km (1,702 miles)

Volga (EUROPE) 3,531km (2,194 miles)

Mississippi (NORTH AMERICA) 3,779 km (2,348 miles)

Chang Jiang (ASIA) 5,530 km (3,436 miles)

Amazon (SOUTH AMERICA) 6,448 km (4,007 miles)

Nile (AFRICA) 6,670 km (4,145 miles)

Deserts
Deserts cover about a seventh of the world's land areas. The Sahara in North Africa is the largest.

Sahara (AFRICA) 8,400,000 sq km (3,250,000 sq miles)

Great Australian Desert (AUSTRALIA) 1,550,000 sq km (600,000 sq miles)

Arabian Desert (ASIA) 1,300,000 sq km (500,000 sq miles)

Gobi Desert (ASIA) 1,170,000 sq km (450,000 sq miles)

Kalahari Desert (AFRICA) 520,000 sq km (200,000 sq miles)

Lakes
The world's largest lake is the Caspian Sea, so called because its water is salty. The largest freshwater lake is Lake Superior.

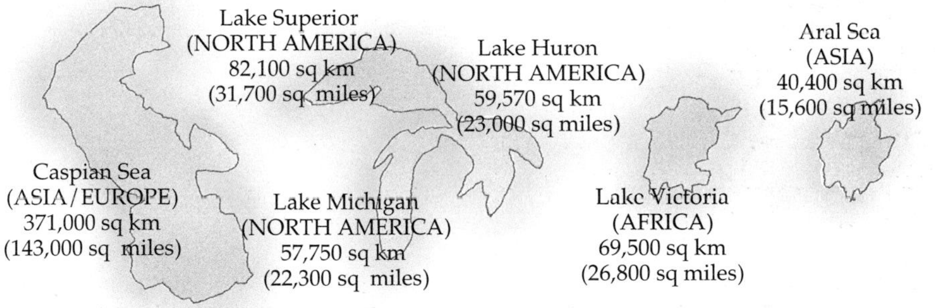

Lake Superior
(NORTH AMERICA)
82,100 sq km
(31,700 sq miles)

Lake Huron
(NORTH AMERICA)
59,570 sq km
(23,000 sq miles)

Aral Sea
(ASIA)
40,400 sq km
(15,600 sq miles)

Caspian Sea
(ASIA / EUROPE)
371,000 sq km
(143,000 sq miles)

Lake Michigan
(NORTH AMERICA)
57,750 sq km
(22,300 sq miles)

Lake Victoria
(AFRICA)
69,500 sq km
(26,800 sq miles)

Islands
Islands are land areas surrounded by water. The world's largest island, Greenland, is mostly covered by ice.

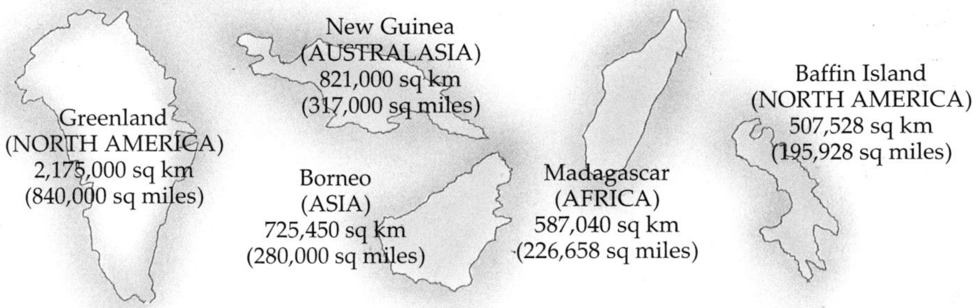

New Guinea
(AUSTRALASIA)
821,000 sq km
(317,000 sq miles)

Baffin Island
(NORTH AMERICA)
507,528 sq km
(195,928 sq miles)

Greenland
(NORTH AMERICA)
2,175,000 sq km
(840,000 sq miles)

Borneo
(ASIA)
725,450 sq km
(280,000 sq miles)

Madagascar
(AFRICA)
587,040 sq km
(226,658 sq miles)

Deeps and depressions
The deepest point on land is the shore of the Dead Sea in Israel and Jordan. The deepest part of the oceans is in the Marianas Trench, in the Pacific.

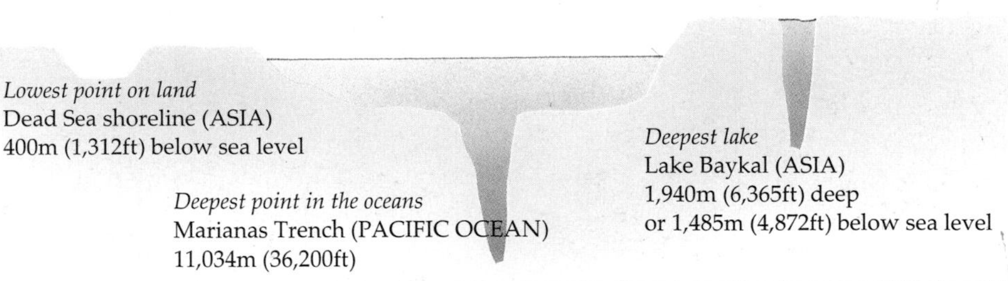

Lowest point on land
Dead Sea shoreline (ASIA)
400m (1,312ft) below sea level

Deepest point in the oceans
Marianas Trench (PACIFIC OCEAN)
11,034m (36,200ft)

Deepest lake
Lake Baykal (ASIA)
1,940m (6,365ft) deep
or 1,485m (4,872ft) below sea level

Measuring the Earth

Models of the Earth are called globes. The surfaces of globes are marked with networks of lines.

Some lines run round the globe. They are called lines of latitude or parallels. The Equator, the Tropics of Cancer and Capricorn, and the Arctic and Antarctic Circles are all lines of latitude.

Other lines on globes run at right angles to the lines of latitude, through both the North and South Poles. These are lines of longitude, or meridians.

Lines of latitude and longitude are marked on maps, which show the globe, or parts of it, on flat pieces of paper. The position of every place on Earth has its own latitude and longitude.

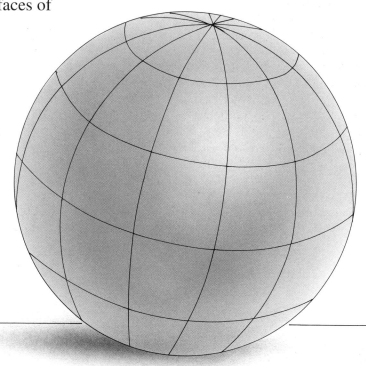

Latitude

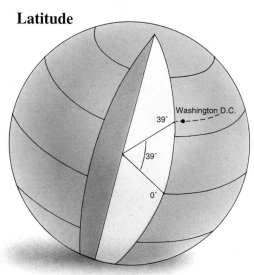

The latitude of the Equator, which divides the Earth into two equal halves, called hemispheres, is 0 degrees. The latitude of the North Pole is 90 degrees North (90°N), while the latitude of the South Pole is 90 degrees South (90°S).

The latitude of places between the Equator and the Poles is measured in degrees north or south of the Equator. For example, the latitude of Washington D.C. is nearly 39 degrees North. This means that the angle formed at the centre of the Earth between the Equator and Washington D.C. is nearly 39 degrees.

The Tropic of Cancer is latitude 23½ degrees North, while the Tropic of Capricorn is 23½ degrees South. The Arctic Circle is 66½ degrees North, while the Antarctic Circle is 66½ degrees South.

Longitude

Lines of longitude are measured 180 degrees east and west of the prime meridian, or 0 degrees longitude. The prime meridian runs through the North Pole, Greenwich, in London, England, and the South Pole. The line was agreed at an international conference in 1884. Washington D.C., for example, is situated at 77 degrees West. This means that the angle formed at the centre of the Earth between the prime meridian and another line of longitude running through Washington D.C. is 77 degrees west of the prime meridian.

The 180 degree line of longitude east and west of the prime meridian runs through the Pacific Ocean, on the far side of the world from the prime meridian. The prime meridian and the 180 degree line of longitude divide the Earth into two hemispheres, east and west, in the same way that the Equator divides north and south.

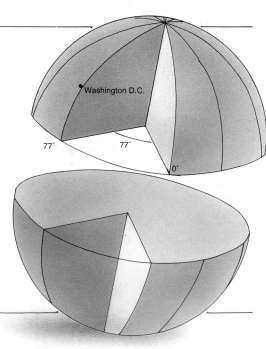

Map projections

One of the problems faced by map-makers is that it is impossible to show the Earth on a flat piece of paper without distorting it to some extent. You can understand the problem if you imagine that the world is an orange. If you peel the orange, there is no way that you can stretch the peel flat without breaking it up and crushing the pieces.

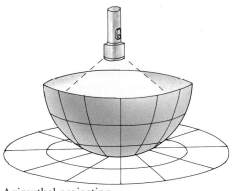

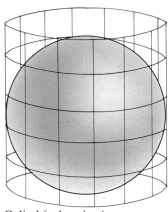

Cylindrical projection

Azimuthal projection

To meet this problem, map-makers use map projections. Imagine a glass globe with the network of lines of latitude and longitude (called graticules) engraved on it. Put a light inside the globe and the graticules will be cast, or projected, on to a flat sheet of paper touching it at one point to produce an *azimuthal projection*. Imagine doing the same with a paper cylinder to produce a *cylindrical projection* or a paper cone to produce a *conical projection*.

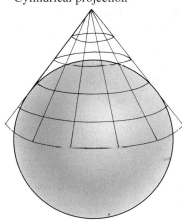

Conical projection

Projections in this atlas

The projections shown above are called perspective projections. But, in practice, map-makers seldom use these projections. Instead, they use projections which they develop using mathematics, so that they can reproduce accurately areas, shapes, distances and directions. Projections used for maps of the world can preserve some of these features, though no single projection can show them all.

The maps that show the continent at the beginning of each chapter of this atlas have been specially drawn to show how the continent looks from space. The map on the right shows how Africa on page 69 would look with lines of latitude and longitude.

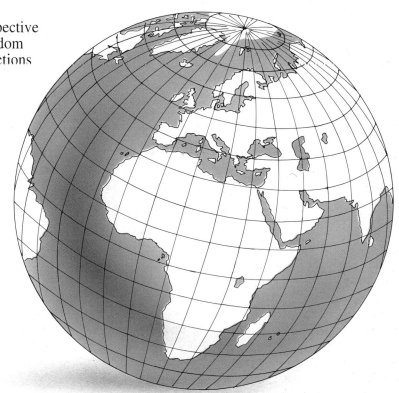

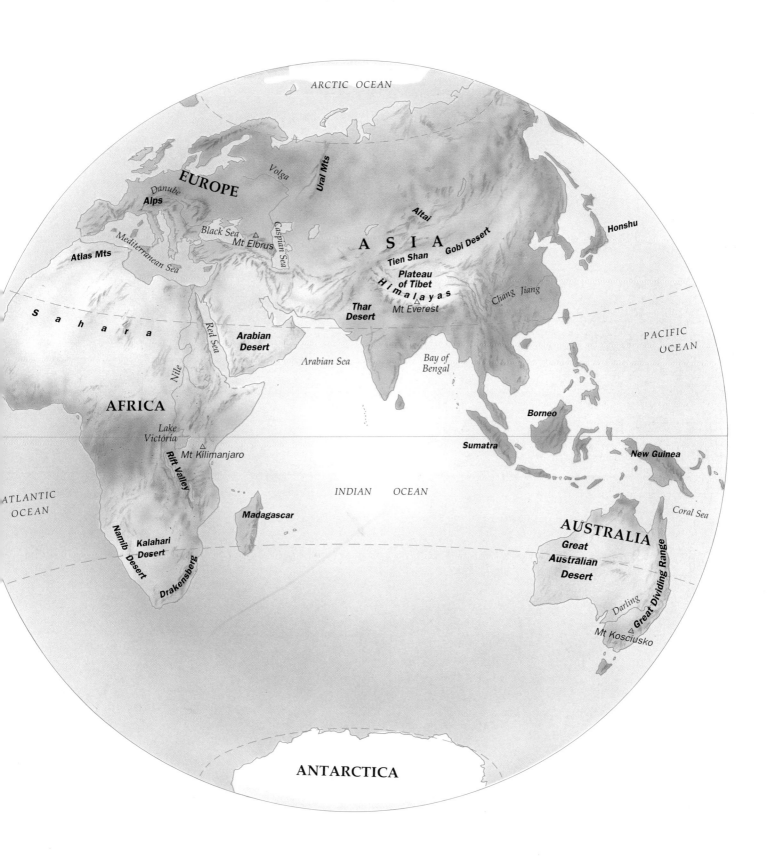

ARCTIC OCEAN

EUROPE

Volga

Ural Mts

ASIA

Danube
Alps

Altai

Honshu

Atlas Mts

Mediterranean Sea

Black Sea
Mt Elbrus

Caspian Sea

Tien Shan

Gobi Desert

Plateau
of Tibet
H i m a l a y a s

Chang Jiang

S a h a r a

Red Sea

Arabian
Desert

Thar
Desert

Mt Everest

PACIFIC
OCEAN

Nile

Arabian Sea

Bay of
Bengal

AFRICA

Lake
Victoria

Rift Valley

Mt Kilimanjaro

Borneo

Sumatra

New Guinea

ATLANTIC
OCEAN

Madagascar

INDIAN   OCEAN

Coral Sea

Namib Desert

Kalahari
Desert

Drakensberg

AUSTRALIA
Great
Australian
Desert

Great Dividing Range

Darling

Mt Kosciusko

ANTARCTICA

The Political World

The world is divided into more than 200 countries. The biggest country is the Russian Federation. The smallest independent country is Vatican City, which covers only 44 hectares (109 acres) in Rome, Italy's capital city.

Most of the world's countries are independent, but some are dependencies – that is, they are ruled by other countries. French Guiana on this map is not an independent country. It is ruled as an overseas region of France.

Most dependencies are tiny island countries. They are so small that they do not appear on this map. The map of the Caribbean on pages 32 and 33 shows several tiny dependencies not shown on this map. They include Montserrat (U.K.), Martinique (France) and the Netherlands Antilles.

1 ANDORRA
2 MONACO
3 LIECHTENSTEIN
4 SAN MARINO
5 VATICAN CITY
6 SLOVENIA
7 CROATIA
8 SERBIA & MONTENEGRO
9 BOSNIA & HERCEGOVINA
10 ALBANIA
11 MACEDONIA

Information panels

This atlas contains panels with information about all the independent countries of the world, including their area, population and capital. Extra details, including information about religions, languages, the economy or main products, and the nature of the government, are given about as many countries as space allows.

Many countries are republics, with a president as head of state. Most republics are democracies, with elected parliaments, though some republics are not democratic.

Other countries are monarchies. Their head of state is a king or queen, though most are actually ruled by elected governments. Some major countries in the Commonwealth, such as Australia, Canada, New Zealand and Britain itself, are constitutional monarchies. They recognize the British queen as their head of state, but in practice democratically elected governments rule these countries.

North America

North America, the third largest continent, contains the world's largest island, Greenland, and three huge countries: Canada, the United States and Mexico. It also includes the smaller countries of Central America and the islands of the Caribbean Sea.

The land of North America includes icy areas in the north and warm tropical places in the south. The United States contain both the Mississippi-Missouri River, North America's longest, and the highest mountain, Mount McKinley in Alaska.

North America contains 23 independent countries. Its total population is about 480 million. Canada and the United States are rich, developed countries. But many people of Central America and the Caribbean are poor.

USA

CANADA

UNITED STATES OF AMERICA

MEXICO

BAHAMAS

ST. CHRISTOPHER & NEVIS

ANTIGUA & BARBUDA

DOMINICAN REPUBLIC

CUBA   HAITI   ST. LUCIA   DOMINICA

ST. VINCENT & GRENADINES   BARBADOS

JAMAICA   GRENADA

TRINIDAD & TOBAGO

BELIZE

GUATEMALA   HONDURAS

EL SALVADOR   NICARAGUA

COSTA RICA   PANAMA

Canada and Greenland

CANADA

Area: 9,976,139 sq km (3,851,809) sq miles); the world's second largest country

Highest point: Mount Logan 6,050m (19,849ft)

Population: 30,491,000

Capital: Ottawa (pop 314,000)

Largest cities:
Toronto (4,263,000)
Montreal (3,326,000)

Official languages: English, French

Religion: Christianity (89.2%)

Main products: Motor vehicles and other manufactures, paper, minerals, farm products

Currency: Canadian Dollar
Government: Constitutional monarchy

ST. PIERRE & MIQUELON

Area: 242 sq km (93 sq miles)

Population: 6,300

Capital: St. Pierre

Government: French territory

C D E F

Ellesmere
Island

Thule

hurst
land

Devon Island

Baffin Bay

Disko
Island

Godhavn

Somerset
Island

nce of
ales
land

Davis Strait

GREENLAND
(DENMARK)

Gunnbjørn △
3700m

Angmagssalik

Frederikshaab

ing
illiam
sland

Baffin
Island

Melville
Peninsula

Godthaab

Cape
Farewell

40°

GREENLAND
Area: 2,175,600 sq km (840,000 sq
miles)
Population: 56,000
Capital: Godthaab (pop 13,400)
Government: Self-governing part
of Denmark

Iqaluit

Frobisher Bay

Southampton
Island

UNAVUT

Hudson Strait

Ungava
Peninsula

Nain

N
E
W
F
O
U
N
D
L
A
N
D

Eskimo Point

Hudson Bay

Labrador

Churchill

Churchill

James
Bay

Fort
Albany

Fort Rupert

Q U E B E C

Anticosti
Island

Corner
Brook

Newfoundland

St John's

MANITOBA

Lake
Winnipeg

St Pierre &
Miquelon
(FRANCE)

ke
nitoba

O N T A R I O

Chicoutimi

NEW
BRUNSWICK

PRINCE
EDWARD ISLAND

Glace Bay

Sydney

Winnipeg

Kenora

Moncton

Charlottetown

NOVA SCOTIA

on

Timmins

St. Lawrence

Quebec

Fredericton

Saint John

Halifax

Thunder Bay

Lake Superior

Sault Ste. Marie

Sudbury

Trois Rivieres

Montreal

Cape Sable

60°

Ottawa

Hull

Ottawa

ATLANTIC OCEAN

Lake
Huron

Peterborough

Kingston

Lake
Michigan

Kitchener

Oshawa

Hamilton

Toronto

Lake
Ontario

London

Niagara Falls

Windsor

Lake Erie

80°

19

United States of America

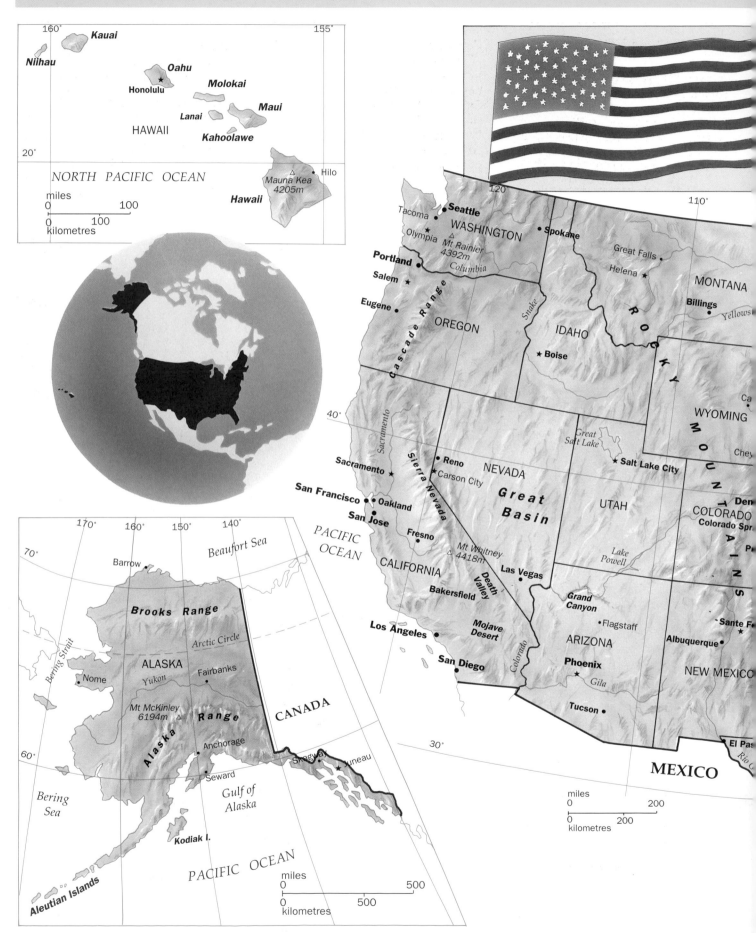

HAWAII

Kauai
Niihau
Oahu
Honolulu
Molokai
Lanai
Maui
Kahoolawe

NORTH PACIFIC OCEAN

Hilo
Mauna Kea 4205m
Hawaii

miles
0   100
0   100
kilometres

ALASKA

Barrow
Beaufort Sea
Brooks Range
Arctic Circle
Bering Strait
Nome
Yukon
Fairbanks
Mt McKinley 6194m
Alaska Range
CANADA
Anchorage
Skagway
Seward
Juneau
Bering Sea
Gulf of Alaska
Kodiak I.
Aleutian Islands
PACIFIC OCEAN

miles
0   500
0   500
kilometres

WASHINGTON
Tacoma
Seattle
Olympia
Spokane
Mt Rainier 4392m
Portland
Columbia
Salem
Eugene
Cascade Range
OREGON
Snake
IDAHO
Boise
Great Falls
Helena
MONTANA
Billings
Yellows
ROCKY
WYOMING
Ca
Chey
Great Salt Lake
Salt Lake City
PACIFIC OCEAN
Sacramento
Reno
Carson City
NEVADA
Great Basin
UTAH
Den
COLORADO
Colorado Spr
San Francisco
Oakland
Sierra Nevada
San Jose
Fresno
Lake Powell
P
Mt Whitney 4418m
Las Vegas
CALIFORNIA
Death Valley
Bakersfield
Grand Canyon
Flagstaff
Sante Fe
Albuquerque
Los Angeles
Mojave Desert
ARIZONA
NEW MEXICO
San Diego
Colorado
Phoenix
Gila
Tucson
El Pas
Rio U
MEXICO

miles
0   200
0   200
kilometres

20

UNITED STATES

Area: 9,529,063 sq km (3,679,192 sq miles); the world's fourth largest country
Highest point: Mount McKinley, Alaska, 6,194m (20,322ft): the highest peak in North America
Population: 281,422,000

Capital: Washington D.C. (pop 572,000)
Largest cities:
New York City (8,008,000)
Los Angeles (3,695,000)
Chicago (2,896,000)
Houston (1,954,000)
Philadelphia (1,518,000)
Official language: English
Religion: Christianity (87.1%)

Economy: *Agriculture:* grains, oil crops, cattle, dairy products; *Mining:* coal, copper, gold, oil, iron, nickel, silver, uranium, zinc; *Industry:* machinery and transport equipment, chemicals, food products
Currency: U.S. Dollar
Government: Federal Republic

USA North-Eastern States

Kentucky

Area: 104,659 sq km (40,410 sq miles)
Population: 4,042,000
Capital: Frankfort (pop 28,000)
Largest city: Lexington (pop 260,000)

West Virginia

Area: 62,758 sq km (24,232 sq miles)
Population: 1,808,000
Capital and largest city: Charleston (pop 53,000)

Virginia

Area: 105,586 sq km (40,767 sq miles)
Population: 7,078,000
Capital: Richmond (pop 198,000)
Largest city: Virginia Beach (pop 425,000)

Pennsylvania

Area: 119,251 sq km (46,043 sq miles)
Population: 12,281,000
Capital: Harrisburg (pop 50,000)
Largest city: Philadelphia (pop 1,518,000)

New York

Area: 136,583 sq km (52,735 sq miles)
Population: 18,976,000
Capital: Albany (pop 96,000)
Largest city: New York City (pop 8,008,000) largest in the USA

Vermont

Area: 24,900 sq km (9,614 sq miles)
Population: 609,000
Capital: Montpelier (pop 8,000)
Largest city: Burlington (pop 39,000)

New Hampshire

Area: 24,032 sq km (9,279 sq miles)
Population: 1,236,000
Capital: Concord (pop 41,000)
Largest city: Manchester (pop 107,000)

Maine

Area: 86,156 sq km (33,265 sq miles)
Population: 1,275,000
Capital: Augusta (pop 19,000)
Largest city: Portland (pop 64,000)

Massachusetts

Area: 21,455 sq km (8,284 sq miles)
Population: 6,349,000
Capital and largest city: Boston (pop 589,000)

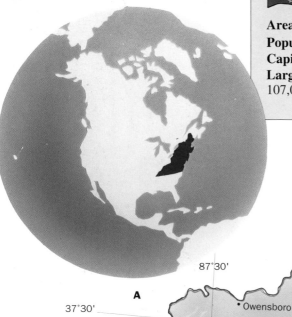

Connecticut

Area: 12,997 sq km (5,018 sq miles)
Population: 3,406,000
Capital: Hartford (pop 122,000)
Largest city: Bridgeport (pop 140,000)

CANADA

Caribou
Presque Isle

I
J
1

Chesuncook Lake
Mt Katahdin △ 1605m
Millinocket

H
Moosehead Lake
MAINE
45°
Eastport

Massena
Ogdensburg
Plattsburgh
Newport
Waterville
Bangor
Bucksport
Mount Desert Island

G
St Lawrence
Lake Champlain
Burlington
Berlin
★ Augusta

F
Mt Marcy △ 1629m
Montpelier
Mt Washington △ 1917m
Auburn Lewiston
2
Adirondack Mts
VERMONT
White Mts
Westbrook
Portland

Watertown
Rutland
NEW HAMPSHIRE
Biddeford

e Ontario
Claremont Rochester
Dover

Glens Falls
Springfield
Concord ★
Portsmouth

Utica
Bennington
Manchester
Nashua Lawrence

ochester
Auburn Syracuse
Mohawk
Troy
Brattleboro
Lowell
Cambridge

Finger Lakes
NEW YORK
Albany
★ Boston
miles
0   100

Ithaca
Pittsfield MASSACHUSETTS
Worcester Brockton
0   100
kilometres

Binghamton
Catskill Mts
Springfield
Cape Cod
3

Hudson
Hartford
Providence ★

Kingston
CONNECTICUT
RHODE ISLAND
Nantucket I.

Scranton
Poughkeepsie
Waterbury
Newport

Williamsport
Wilkes-Barre
New Haven
Martha's Vineyard

Susquehanna
Bridgeport
Stamford

e College
Sunbury
Paterson
Long Island
ATLANTIC OCEAN

PENNSYLVANIA
Bethlehem
Newark
Jersey City
New York City

ona
Allentown
Elizabeth
NEW JERSEY

Harrisburg
Reading
★ Trenton

Lancaster
Norristown
Levittown

York
Philadelphia
Camden

Chambersburg
Wilmington

Hagerstown
Newark
Atlantic City

sburg
Frederick
Vineland

Winchester
Baltimore
Dover
Cape May

MARYLAND
Milford

Washington DC ★
Annapolis
DELAWARE
4

Arlington
Alexandria

nburg
Lexington Park
Salisbury

ericksburg
5

arlottesville
Cape May

NIA
James
Richmond ★

Petersburg
Hampton
Newport News
Norfolk
Portsmouth
Virginia Beach

Chesapeake Bay

Rhode Island

Area: 3,139 sq km (1,212 sq miles)
Population: 1,048,000
Capital and largest city: Providence (pop 174,000)

Maryland

Area: 27,091 sq km (10,460 sq miles)
Population: 5,296,000
Capital: Annapolis (pop 36,000)
Largest city: Baltimore (pop 651,000)

Delaware

Area: 5,294 sq km (2,045 sq miles)
Population: 784,000
Capital: Dover (pop 32,000)
Largest city: Wilmington (pop 73,000)

Washington D.C.

Washington D.C., capital of the USA, is a federal district and is not part of a state. The D.C. stands for District of Columbia. Washington D.C. has an area of 179 sq km (69 sq miles) and a population of 572,000.

New Jersey

Area: 20,168 sq km (7,787 sq miles)
Population: 8,414,000
Capital: Trenton (pop 85,000)
Largest city: Newark (pop 274,000)

USA South-Eastern States

 Texas

Area: 691,207 sq km
(266,807 sq miles)
Population: 20,852,000
Capital: Austin (pop 657,000)
Largest city: Houston
(pop 1,954,000)

 Oklahoma

Area: 181,185 sq km
(69,955 sq miles)
Population: 3,450,000
Capital and largest city:
Oklahoma City (pop 506,000)

Arkansas

Area: 137,754 sq km
(53,187 sq miles)
Population: 2,673,000
Capital and largest city:
Little Rock (pop 183,000)

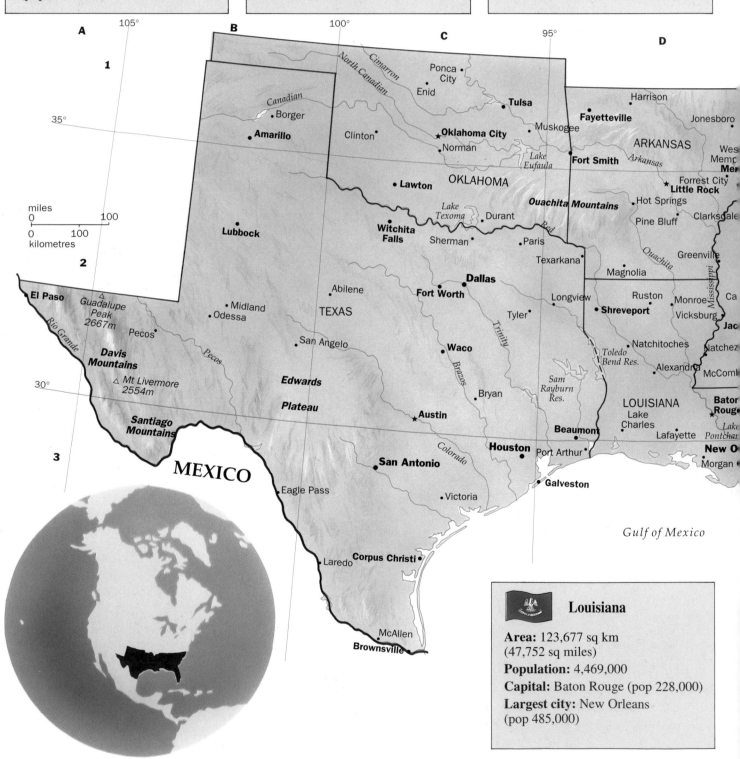

Louisiana

Area: 123,677 sq km
(47,752 sq miles)
Population: 4,469,000
Capital: Baton Rouge (pop 228,000)
Largest city: New Orleans
(pop 485,000)

Tennessee

Area: 109,152 sq km
(42,144 sq miles)
Population: 5,689,000
Capital: Nashville (pop 570,000)
Largest city: Memphis
(pop 650,000)

North Carolina

Area: 136,412 sq km
(52,669 sq miles)
Population: 8,049,000
Capital: Raleigh (pop 276,000)
Largest city: Charlotte
(pop 541,000)

South Carolina

Area: 80,582 sq km
(31,113 sq miles)
Population: 4,012,000
Capital and largest city:
Columbia (pop 116,000)

Alabama

Area: 133,915 sq km
(51,705 sq miles)
Population: 4,447,000
Capital: Montgomery
(pop 202,000)
Largest city: Birmingham
(pop 243,000)

Georgia

Area: 152,576 sq km
(58,910 sq miles)
Population: 8,186,000
Capital and largest city:
Atlanta (pop 416,000)

Florida

Area: 151,939 sq km
(58,664 sq miles)
Population: 15,982,000
Capital: Tallahassee (pop 150,000)
Largest city: Jacksonville
(pop 736,000)

Mississippi

Area: 123,514 sq km
(47,689 sq miles)
Population: 2,845,000
Capital and largest city:
Jackson (pop 184,000)

USA Mid-Western States

 North Dakota

Area: 183,117 sq km (70,702 sq miles)
Population: 642,000
Capital: Bismarck (pop 55,000)
Largest city: Fargo (pop 90,000)

 South Dakota

Area: 199,730 sq km (77,116 sq miles)
Population: 755,000
Capital: Pierre (pop 14,000)
Largest city: Sioux Falls (pop 124,000)

 Minnesota

Area: 224,329 sq km (86,614 sq miles)
Population: 4,919,000
Capital: St. Paul (pop 287,000)
Largest city: Minneapolis (pop 383,000)

 Nebraska

Area: 200,349 sq km (77,355 sq miles)
Population: 1,711,000
Capital: Lincoln (pop 226,000)
Largest city: Omaha (pop 390,000)

 Kansas

Area: 213,096 sq km (82,277 sq miles)
Population: 2,688,000
Capital: Topeka (pop 122,000)
Largest city: Wichita (pop 344,000)

Iowa

Area: 145,752 sq km (56,275 sq miles)
Population: 2,926,000
Capital and largest city: Des Moines (pop 199,000)

 Missouri

Area: 180,514 sq km (69,697 sq miles)
Population: 5,595,000
Capital: Jefferson City (pop 40,000)
Largest city: Kansas City (pop 442,000)

 Wisconsin

Area: 171,496 sq km (66,215 sq miles)
Population: 5,364,000
Capital: Madison (pop 208,000)
Largest city: Milwaukee (pop 597,000)

 Michigan

Area: 251,493 sq km (97,102 sq miles)
Population: 9,938,000
Capital: Lansing (pop 119,000)
Largest city: Detroit (pop 951,000)

 Ohio

Area: 115,998 sq km (44,787 sq miles)
Population: 11,353,000
Capital and largest city: Columbus (pop 711,000)

 Indiana

Area: 94,309 sq km (36,413 sq miles)
Population: 6,080,000
Capital and largest city: Indianapolis (pop 792,000)

 Illinois

Area: 149,885 sq km (57,871 sq miles)
Population: 12,419,000
Capital: Springfield (pop 111,000)
Largest city: Chicago (pop 2,896,000)

USA Western States

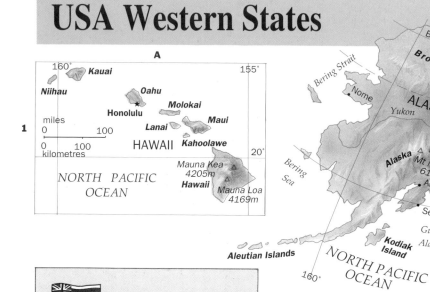

A

160° **Kauai**   155°
Niihau
Oahu
Honolulu **Molokai**
miles   **Lanai** **Maui**
0   100
0   100   **Kahoolawe**
kilometres   HAWAII   20°

NORTH PACIFIC
OCEAN

Mauna Kea
4205m
Hawaii Mauna Loa
4169m

1

Barrow
Brooks Range
Beaufort Sea 70°
Bering Strait
Nome ALASKA
Arctic Circle
Yukon
Fairbanks
Alaska Range
Mt McKinley
6194m
Anchorage
Seward
Skagway
Juneau
60°
Bering Sea
Kodiak Island
Gulf of Alaska
Sitka
Aleutian Islands
NORTH PACIFIC
OCEAN
160° 140°

miles
0   200
0   200
kilometres

C
Bellingham
Everett
Bremerton Seattle
Aberdeen **Tacoma**
Olympia Yakima
WASHI
Mt Rainier
4392m
Portland Columbia Ken
Salem
Corvallis John Day River
Colum
Eugene Plate
Bend
OREGON
Coos Bay
Medford
Klamath Falls
Eureka
Sacramento
Chico
Reno
Sparks
Carson City
Santa Rosa **Sacramento**
Lake Tahoe
San Francisco **Oakland** Stockton
San Joaquin
San Jose
Monterey Fresno
Visalia Mt 4
CALIFORNIA
Santa Maria
Santa Barbara
San Bernardino
PACIFIC OCEAN Los Angeles Ana
Long Beach Sa
Channel Islands
San Dieg

45°
40°
35°
1
2
3
4

miles
0   200
0   200
kilometres

Hawaii

Area: 16,760 sq km (6,471 sq miles)
Population: 1,212,000
Capital and largest city: Honolulu (pop 372,000)

Alaska

Area: 1,530,693 sq km (591,004 sq miles)
Population: 627,000
Capital: Juneau (pop 31,000)
Largest city: Anchorage (pop 260,000)

Washington

Area: 176,479 sq km (68,139 sq miles)
Population: 5,894,000
Capital: Olympia (pop 42,000)
Largest city: Seattle (pop 563,000)

Idaho

Area: 216,430 sq km (83,564 sq miles)
Population: 1,294,000
Capital and largest city: Boise (pop 186,000)

Oregon

Area: 251,418 sq km (97,073 sq miles)
Population: 3,421,000
Capital: Salem (pop 137,000)
Largest city: Portland (pop 529,000)

Nevada

Area: 286,352 sq km (110,561 sq miles)
Population: 1,998,000
Capital: Carson City (pop 52,000)
Largest city: Las Vegas (pop 478,000)

California

Area: 411,047 sq km (158,706 sq miles)
Population: 33,872,000 (California has a larger population than any other state in the United States)
Capital: Sacramento (pop 407,000)
Largest city: Los Angeles (pop 3,695,000)

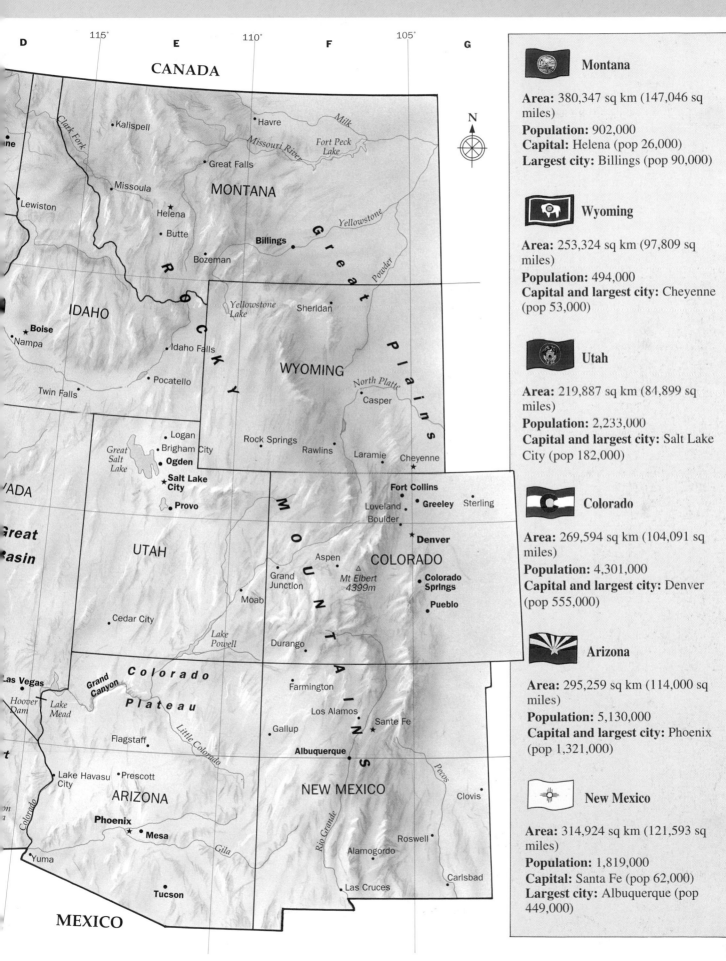

CANADA

D   115°   E   110°   F   105°   G

N

Kalispell
Clark Fork
Havre
Milk
Missouri River
Fort Peck Lake
Great Falls
Missoula
MONTANA
Lewiston
Helena
Butte
Billings
Bozeman
Yellowstone
Powder
IDAHO
R
Yellowstone Lake
Sheridan
Great
Boise
Nampa
Idaho Falls
WYOMING
Pocatello
North Platte
Twin Falls
Casper
Logan
Rock Springs
Rawlins
Brigham City
Great Salt Lake
Ogden
Laramie
Cheyenne
Salt Lake City
Plains
O
Fort Collins
Loveland Greeley Sterling
Provo
Boulder
VADA
M
Denver
Great Basin
UTAH
Aspen
COLORADO
Grand Junction
Mt Elbert 4399m
Colorado Springs
Moab
Pueblo
Cedar City
Lake Powell
Durango
U
Las Vegas
Grand Canyon
Colorado
Plateau
Farmington
Hoover Dam
Lake Mead
Los Alamos
Gallup
Sante Fe
Flagstaff
Little Colorado
Albuquerque
T
Lake Havasu City
Prescott
Pecos
ARIZONA
NEW MEXICO
Clovis
Colorado
Phoenix
Mesa
Rio Grande
Roswell
Yuma
Gila
Alamogordo
Tucson
Carlsbad
Las Cruces

MEXICO

Montana

Area: 380,347 sq km (147,046 sq miles)
Population: 902,000
Capital: Helena (pop 26,000)
Largest city: Billings (pop 90,000)

Wyoming

Area: 253,324 sq km (97,809 sq miles)
Population: 494,000
Capital and largest city: Cheyenne (pop 53,000)

Utah

Area: 219,887 sq km (84,899 sq miles)
Population: 2,233,000
Capital and largest city: Salt Lake City (pop 182,000)

Colorado

Area: 269,594 sq km (104,091 sq miles)
Population: 4,301,000
Capital and largest city: Denver (pop 555,000)

Arizona

Area: 295,259 sq km (114,000 sq miles)
Population: 5,130,000
Capital and largest city: Phoenix (pop 1,321,000)

New Mexico

Area: 314,924 sq km (121,593 sq miles)
Population: 1,819,000
Capital: Santa Fe (pop 62,000)
Largest city: Albuquerque (pop 449,000)

Mexico and Central America

A 115° **B** 110° **C** 105° **D** 100° **E**

Tijuana
Mexicali
Ensenada
Colorado
1
30°

Ciudad
Juárez

UNITED STATES

N

Hermosillo
Gulf of California
Chihuahua
Rio Bravo del Norte
Piedras
Negras
2
Baja California
Ciudad Obrégon
• Hidalgo Del Parral
Nuevo
Laredo

Sierra Madre Occidental

Los Mochis
• Guasave
Torreón
Monterrey
Reynosa
Matamoros
25°
Saltillo

Culiacán
M E X I C O
Sierra Madre Oriental

• Durango
• Ciudad Victori

Mazatlán
3

Aguascalientes
San Luis
Potosi
Tampi

• Tepic
• León
Guadalajara
Irapuato•
Querétaro
Celaya
Pachuca
20°
Uruapan
Mexico City
Citlaltépetl
J E
• Colima
Morelia
Volcano
5700m
Toluca
Ver
Cuernavaca
Puebla
Or
PACIFIC
Balsas
Popocatépetl
Volcano 5452m
4
OCEAN

Sierra Madre del Sur
Oax
Acapulco

15°

MEXICO

Area: 1,972,547 sq km (761,605 sq
miles)

Highest point: Citlaltépetl (also
called Orizaba) 5,700m (18,701ft)

Population: 96,586,000

Capital and largest city: Mexico
City (pop 8,520,000; pop of
metropolitan area 16,764,000)

Other cities:
Guadalajara (3,461,000)
Monterrey (3,022,000)
Puebla (1,561,000)

Official language: Spanish

Religion: Christianity (95.9%)

Main products: Oil, silver,
machinery and other manufactures,
farm products

Currency: Mexican Peso

Government: Federal republic
(official name: United States of
Mexico)

BELIZE

Area: 22,965 sq km (8,867 sq
miles)

Population: 247,000

Capital: Belmopan (pop 6,500)

Largest city: Belize City (pop
50,000)

GUATEMALA
Area: 108,889 sq km (42,042 sq miles)
Population: 11,088,000
Capital and largest city: Guatemala City (pop 1,167,000)
Currency: Quetzal

EL SALVADOR
Area: 21,041 sq km (8,124 sq miles)
Population: 6,154,000
Capital and largest city: San Salvador (pop 442,000)
Official language: Spanish
Currency: Colón, U.S. Dollar

HONDURAS
Area: 112,088 sq km (43,277 sq miles)
Population: 6,318,000
Capital and largest city: Tegucigalpa (pop 919,000)
Currency: Lempira

NICARAGUA
Area: 130,000 sq km (50,193 sq miles)
Population: 4,919,000
Capital and largest city: Managua (pop 930,000)
Official language: Spanish
Currency: Córdoba

COSTA RICA
Area: 50,700 sq km (19,575 sq miles)
Population: 3,589,000
Capital and largest city: San José (pop 346,000)
Official language: Spanish
Currency: Colón

PANAMA
Area: 77,082 sq km (29,762 sq miles)
Population: 2,811,000
Capital and largest city: Panama City (pop 658,000)
Official language: Spanish
Currency: Balboa

F 90° G

Gulf of Mexico

Tropic of Cancer

• **Mérida**

Campeche •   **Yucatán Peninsula**

Campeche Bay

Villahermosa
acoalcos

Tuxtla
• **Gutiérrez**

• Belize City

☐ Belmopan

BELIZE

GUATEMALA
Quezaltenango

Tapachula

Guatemala City
Santa Ana

EL SALVADOR

85°   H

Gulf of Honduras

Caribbean Sea

• **San Pedro Sula**

HONDURAS
Tegucigalpa ☐

☐ **San Salvador**
• **San Miguel**

León

NICARAGUA

Managua ☐
Granada

Lake Nicaragua

80°   I

10°

COSTA RICA

San José ☐

Colón •
Panama Canal   **Panama City** ☐

David   **PANAMA**   *Gulf of Panama*

miles
0   200
0   200
kilometres

5

6

31

Caribbean

CUBA
Area: 110,861 sq km (42,804 sq miles)
Population: 11,178,000
Capital: Havana (pop 2,242,000)

JAMAICA
Area: 10,991 sq km (4,244 sq miles)
Population: 2,598,000
Capital: Kingston (pop 655,000)

BAHAMAS
Area: 13,935 sq km (5,380 sq miles)
Population: 298,000
Capital: Nassau (pop 214,000)

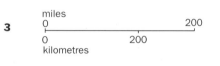

PUERTO RICO
Area: 8,897 sq km (3,435 sq miles)
Population: 3,890,000
Capital: San Juan (pop 439,000)

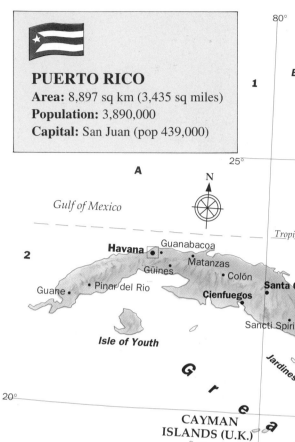

80°   B   7
Grand Bahama I.   Little Abaco I.
Freeport   Great Abaco I.
25°
Eleuthera I.
New Providence I.
Nassau
Andros town
Cat I.
Andros I.   BAHAMAS
Great Exuma I.   Salva
A
N
Gulf of Mexico
Long I.
Cro
Tropic of Cancer
Ragge
2
Havana   Guanabacoa
Güines   Matanzas
Guane   Pinar del Rio   Colón   Santa Clara   Camagüey Arch.
Cienfuegos
Morón
Sancti Spiritus   Ciego de Avila
Isle of Youth
CUBA   Camagüey
Victoria de las Tunas   Holguin
Jardines de la Reina   Manzanillo   Bayamo
20°
Pico Turquino   Guantán
CAYMAN ISLANDS (U.K.)   △1974m
George Town   Santiago de Cuba
Greater

miles
0   200
3
0   200
kilometres

Montego Bay   JAMAICA
Mandeville
Spanish Town   Kingston
An

Caribbean Sea

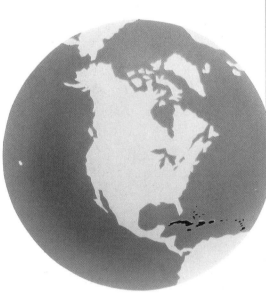

DOMINICAN REPUBLIC
Area: 48,734 sq km (18,816 sq miles)
Population: 8,404,000
Capital and largest city: Santo Domingo (pop 1,600,000)
Official language: Spanish
Religion: Christianity
Main products: Sugar, gold, silver, coffee, cocoa
Currency: Peso

HAITI
Area: 27,750 sq km (10,714 sq miles)
Population: 7,803,000
Capital and largest city: Port-au-Prince (pop 917,000)
Official language: French
Religion: Christianity
Currency: Gourde

ANTIGUA AND BARBUDA
Area: 440 sq km (170 sq miles)
Population: 67,000
Capital: Saint John's (pop 25,000)

DOMINICA
Area: 751 sq km (290 sq miles)
Population: 73,000
Capital: Roseau (pop 24,000)

ST. CHRISTOPHER-NEVIS
Area: 261 sq km (101 sq miles)
Population: 41,000
Capital: Basseterre (pop 12,600)

ST. LUCIA
Area: 616 sq km (238 sq miles)
Population: 154,000
Capital: Castries (pop 57,000)

ST. VINCENT & THE GRENADINES
Area: 388 sq km (150 sq miles)
Population: 114,000
Capital: Kingstown (pop 28,000)

FRENCH CARIBBEAN TERRITORIES:
Guadeloupe, Martinique

NETHERLANDS TERRITORIES:
Aruba, Netherlands Antilles

BRITISH TERRITORIES:
Anguilla, Cayman Islands, Montserrat, Turks and Caicos Islands, Virgin Islands

U.S. TERRITORIES:
Virgin Islands

C 70°
Mayaguana I.

TURKS & CAICOS ISLANDS (U.K.)
Grand Turk

ew Town

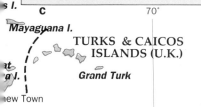

Cap-Haïtien   Puerto Plata
ives   **Santiago.**   DOMINICAN
• St Marc   • La Vega   REPUBLIC
Port-au-Prince   Azua   La Romana
yes   Jacmel   **Santo Domingo**
Barahona

l l e s

D   *ATLANTIC OCEAN*   65°   E   F

60°

VIRGIN ISLANDS (U.S.) (U.K.)   ANGUILLA (U.K.)
Arecibo   **San Juan**   Road Town
Mayaguez   **Ponce**   Charlotte   **St. Martin**
Amalie   ANTIGUA AND BARBUDA
PUERTO RICO (U.S.)   Basseterre   St John's
ST CHRISTOPHER-NEVIS   MONTSERRAT (U.K.)
Plymouth   GUADELOUPE (Fr.)
Basse Terre   DOMINICA
Roseau
15°   MARTINIQUE (Fr.)
Fort-de-France   Castries   ST LUCIA
BARBADOS
Kingstown   Bridgetown
4   ST VINCENT & THE GRENADINES
St George's   GRENADA
Tobago
Scarborough
Port of Spain   TRINIDAD AND TOBAGO
10°   **Trinidad**

GRENADA
Area: 344 sq km (133 sq miles)
Population: 97,000
Capital: St George's (pop 35,000)

NETHERLANDS ANTLLES
Aruba   *Bonaire*
Curaçao   Willemstad

BARBADOS
Area: 431 sq km (166 sq miles)
Population: 267,000
Capital: Bridgetown (pop 6,000)

TRINIDAD AND TOBAGO
Area: 5,130 sq km (1,981 sq miles)
Population: 1,293,000
Capital: Port of Spain (pop 53,000)

South America

South America is the fourth largest continent. It includes Brazil, a country which is larger than Australia. Much of the continent has a warm climate and forests cover large areas of the north. Deserts border the coasts of west-central South America. Patagonia, in Argentina, is a dry, cold region.

The Andes Mountains, the world's largest mountain range, contain Aconcagua, South America's highest peak. The longest river is the Amazon.

South America includes 12 independent countries, French Guiana which is ruled as part of France, and the Falkland Islands, which are ruled by Britain. South America has about 340 million people. A few people are wealthy, but the great majority are poor.

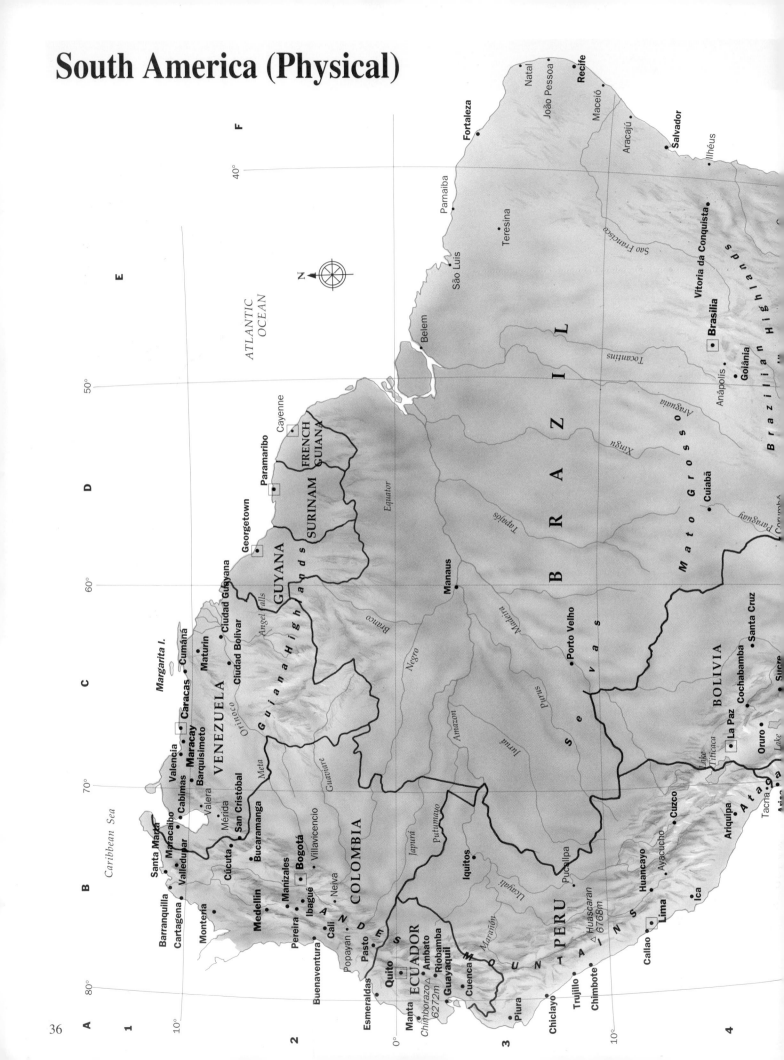

South America (Physical)

ATLANTIC OCEAN

N

Caribbean Sea

Margarita I.

VENEZUELA

Barranquilla
Cartagena
Santa Marta
Maracaibo
Valledupar
Cabimas
Valencia
Valera
Mérida
Barquisimeto
Maracay
Caracas
Cumaná
Maturín
Ciudad Guayana
Ciudad Bolívar
San Cristóbal
Bucaramanga
Cúcuta

Orinoco
Meta

Cayenne
Paramaribo
Georgetown

FRENCH GUIANA
SURINAM
GUYANA

Guiana Highlands
Angel Falls

Equator

Branco
Negro

COLOMBIA

Montería
Medellín
Manizales
Pereira
Ibagué
Bogotá
Villavicencio
Cali
Popayán
Neiva
Buenaventura
Pasto

Guaviare
Putumayo
Japurá
Caquetá

ECUADOR
Esmeraldas
Manta
Quito
Ambato
Chimborazo 6272m
Riobamba
Guayaquil
Cuenca

A N D E S

Napo
Marañón

Piura
Chiclayo
Trujillo
Chimbote

PERU
Iquitos
Pucallpa

Ucayali
Juruá
Purus
Madre de Dios

Callao
Lima
Ica
Huancayo
Ayacucho
Cuzco
Huascaran 6768m

Arequipa
Tacna

BOLIVIA
La Paz
Oruro
Cochabamba
Santa Cruz
Sucre

Lake Titicaca

Atacama

B R A Z I L

Amazon
Manaus
Porto Velho
Madeira
Tapajós
Xingu
Araguaia
Tocantins

S e l v a s

Mato Grosso

Cuiabá
Corumbá
Paraguay

Belém
São Luís
Parnaíba
Teresina
Fortaleza

Natal
João Pessoa
Recife
Maceió
Aracajú
Salvador
Ilhéus

São Francisco
Brazilian Highlands

Vitória da Conquista
Brasília
Anápolis
Goiânia

M O U N T A I N S

36

PACIFIC OCEAN

SOUTH
ATLANTIC
OCEAN

miles
0
kilometres
0
500
500

PARAGUAY

Concepción

Asunción

Posadas

Corrientes

Resistencia

Gran Chaco

Salta

San Miguel de
Tucumán

Santiago
del Estero

Córdoba

Santa Fe

Paraná

Rosario

Rio Cuarto

San Juan

Mendoza

Aconcagua 6960m

ARGENTINA

Pampa

Buenos Aires

La Plata

Tandil

Bahia Blanca

Mar del Plata

Colorado

Negro

Patagonia

Chubut

Deseado

Comodoro Rivadavia

Uruguay

Rivera

Bagé

Salto

Paysandu

URUGUAY

Montevideo

Santa Maria

Uruguaiana

Pelotas

Passo Fundo

Ponta Grossa

Pôrto Alegre

Florianopolis

Blumenau

Curitiba

Sorocaba

Bauru

Prudente

Campinas

São Paulo

Santos

Rio de Janeiro

Volta Redonda

Tropic of Capricorn

Antofagasta

La Serena

CHILE

Viña del Mar
Valparaiso

Santiago

Rancagua

Talca

Chillán

Talcahuanco
Concepción

Temuco

Valdivia

Osorno

Puerto Montt

Desert

MOUNTAINS

ANDES

San Félix I.
(Chile) San Ambrosio I.
(Chile)

Juan Fernández Is. (Chile)

Strait of Magellan

Punta Arenas

Tierra del Fuego

Ushuaia

Cape Horn

Falkland Islands (U.K.)

Stanley

30°

40°

50°

5
6
7
8

South America (Political)

COLOMBIA
Area: 1,138,914 sq km (439,747 sq miles)
Population: 41,530,000
Capital and largest city: Bogotá (pop 6,276,000)
Currency: Colombian Peso

VENEZUELA
Area: 912,050 sq km (352,145 sq miles)
Population: 23,707,000
Capital and largest city: Caracas (pop 1,964,000)
Currency: Bolivar

ECUADOR
Area: 283,561 sq km (109,484 sq miles)
Population: 12,412,000
Capital: Quito (pop 1,376,000)
Currency: U.S. Dollar

PERU
Area: 1,285,216 sq km (496,225 sq miles)
Population: 25,230,000
Capital and largest city: Lima (pop 6,464,000)
Currency: Sol

BOLIVIA
Area: 1,098,581 sq km (424,165 sq miles)
Population: 8,138,000
Capital and largest city: La Paz (pop 1,004,000)
Currency: Boliviano

CHILE
Area: 756,945 sq km (292,258 sq miles)
Population: 15,018,000
Capital and largest city: Santiago (pop 4,640,000)
Currency: Chilean Peso

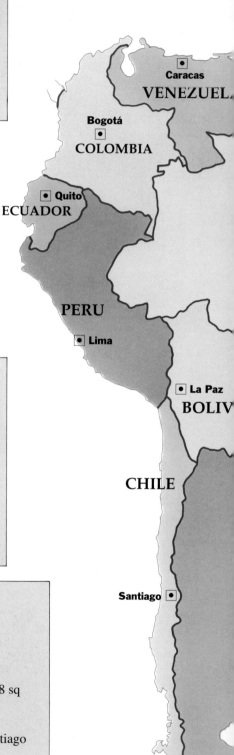

Caracas
VENEZUELA
Bogotá
COLOMBIA
Quito
ECUADOR
PERU
Lima
La Paz
BOLIV
CHILE
Santiago

GUYANA
Area: 214,969 sq km (83,000 sq miles)
Population: 856,000
Capital: Georgetown (pop 275,000)
Currency: Guyana Dollar

SURINAM
Area: 163,265 sq km (63,037 sq miles)
Population: 413,000
Capital: Paramaribo (pop 289,000)
Currency: Surinam Guilder

FRENCH GUIANA
Area: 90,000 sq km (34,749 sq miles)
Population: 157,000
Capital: Cayenne (pop 50,000)
Currency: Euro

BRAZIL
Area: 8,511,965 sq km (3,286,488 sq miles)
Population: 167,967,000
Capital: Brasilia (pop 1,566,000)
Largest cities: São Paulo (16,583,000) metropolitan area) Rio de Janeiro (10,192,000) Belo Horizonte (3,803,000)
Official language: Portuguese
Currency: Cruzeiro

PARAGUAY
Area: 406,752 sq km (157,048 sq miles)
Population: 5,359,000
Capital and largest city: Asunción (pop 501,000)
Official language: Spanish
Currency: Guarani

ARGENTINA
Area: 2,766,889 sq km (1,068,302 sq miles)
Highest point: Aconcagua 6,960m (22,831ft)
Population: 36,580,000
Capital and largest city: Buenos Aires (pop 2,982,000; metropolitan area 11,802,000)
Official language: Spanish
Religion: Christianity
Currency: Argentine Peso

URUGUAY
Area: 176,215 sq km (68,037 sq miles)
Population: 3,313,000
Capital and largest city: Montevideo (pop 1,237,000)
Currency: New Peso

FALKLAND ISLANDS (U.K.)
Area: 12,173 sq km (4,700 sq miles)
Population: 2,500
Capital: Stanley

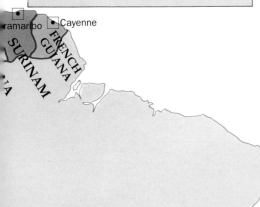

Paramaribo
Cayenne
town

BRAZIL

Brasilia

PARAGUAY
Asunción

URUGUAY
Montevideo

ARGENTINA

kland Islands (U.K.)

Stanley

Europe

Europe is the second smallest continent; only Australia is smaller. It contains parts of the former Soviet Union including Belarus, Moldova, Ukraine, Estonia, Latvia, Lithuania and part of the Russian Federation, the world's largest country and the only country located in more than one continent.

The highest peak in Europe is Mount Elbrus in the Caucasus Mountains which form part of the border between Europe and Asia. The longest river, the Volga, is in the Russian Federation and flows into the Caspian Sea.

Europe also contains the world's smallest country, Vatican City, which is situated in Rome, the capital of Italy.

Europe's population of about 700 million, including the European part of Russia, is greater than that of any other continent except Asia and Africa.

41

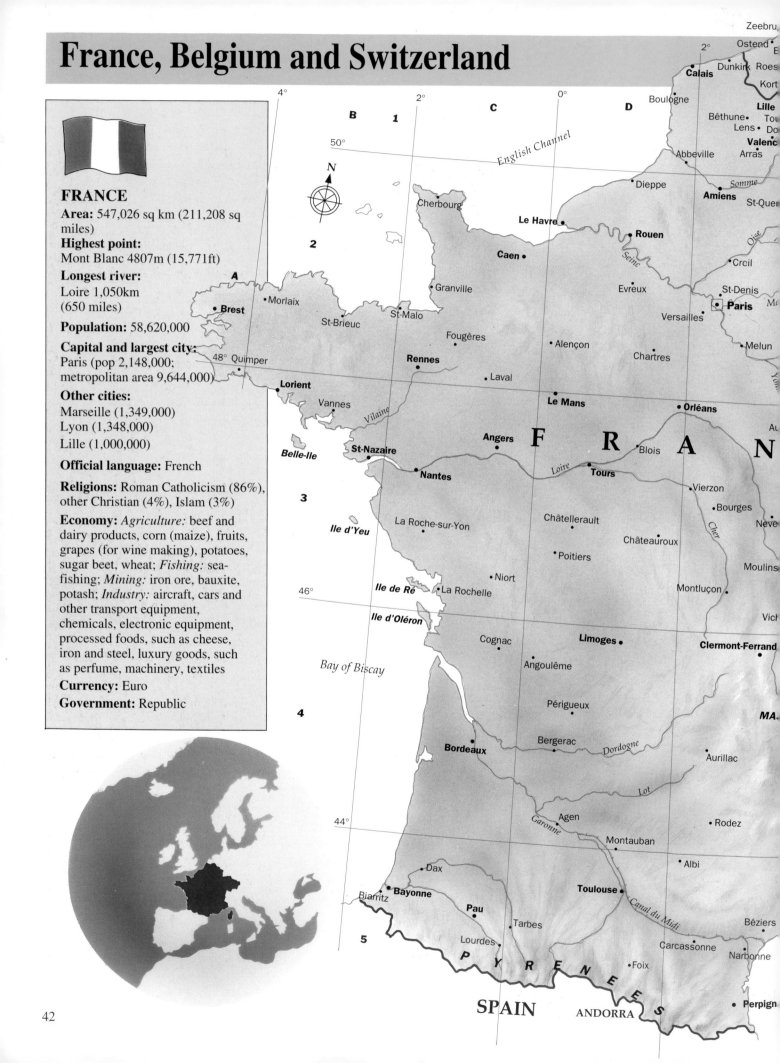

FRANCE

Area: 547,026 sq km (211,208 sq miles)

Highest point: Mont Blanc 4807m (15,771ft)

Longest river: Loire 1,050km (650 miles)

Population: 58,620,000

Capital and largest city: Paris (pop 2,148,000; metropolitan area 9,644,000)

Other cities:
Marseille (1,349,000)
Lyon (1,348,000)
Lille (1,000,000)

Official language: French

Religions: Roman Catholicism (86%), other Christian (4%), Islam (3%)

Economy: *Agriculture:* beef and dairy products, corn (maize), fruits, grapes (for wine making), potatoes, sugar beet, wheat; *Fishing:* sea-fishing; *Mining:* iron ore, bauxite, potash; *Industry:* aircraft, cars and other transport equipment, chemicals, electronic equipment, processed foods, such as cheese, iron and steel, luxury goods, such as perfume, machinery, textiles

Currency: Euro

Government: Republic

English Channel

Zeebru
Ostend
Calais
Dunkirk Roes
Kort
Boulogne
Lille
Béthune Tou
Lens Do
Valenc
Abbeville Arras
Dieppe
Somme
Amiens St-Quer
Cherbourg
Le Havre
Rouen
Caen
Crcil
Granville
Evreux
St-Denis
Paris
Versailles
Melun
Morlaix
Brest
Fougères
Alençon
Chartres
St-Brieuc St-Malo
Rennes
Laval
Le Mans
Orléans
Au
Quimper
Lorient
Vannes
Angers
F R A N
Blois
Vilaine
Vierzon
Belle-Ile
St-Nazaire
Loire Tours
Bourges
Nantes
Neve
Châtellerault
Cher
Ile d'Yeu
La Roche-sur-Yon
Châteauroux
Moulins
Poitiers
Niort
Montluçon
Ile de Ré
La Rochelle
Vich
Ile d'Oléron
Cognac
Limoges
Clermont-Ferrand
Angoulême
MA.
Bay of Biscay
Périgueux
Aurillac
Bordeaux
Bergerac
Dordogne
Lot
Rodez
Agen
Garonne
Montauban
Albi
Dax
Toulouse
Biarritz Bayonne
Canal du Midi
Béziers
Pau
Tarbes
Carcassonne
Narbonne
Lourdes
Foix
P Y R E N E E S
Perpign
SPAIN ANDORRA

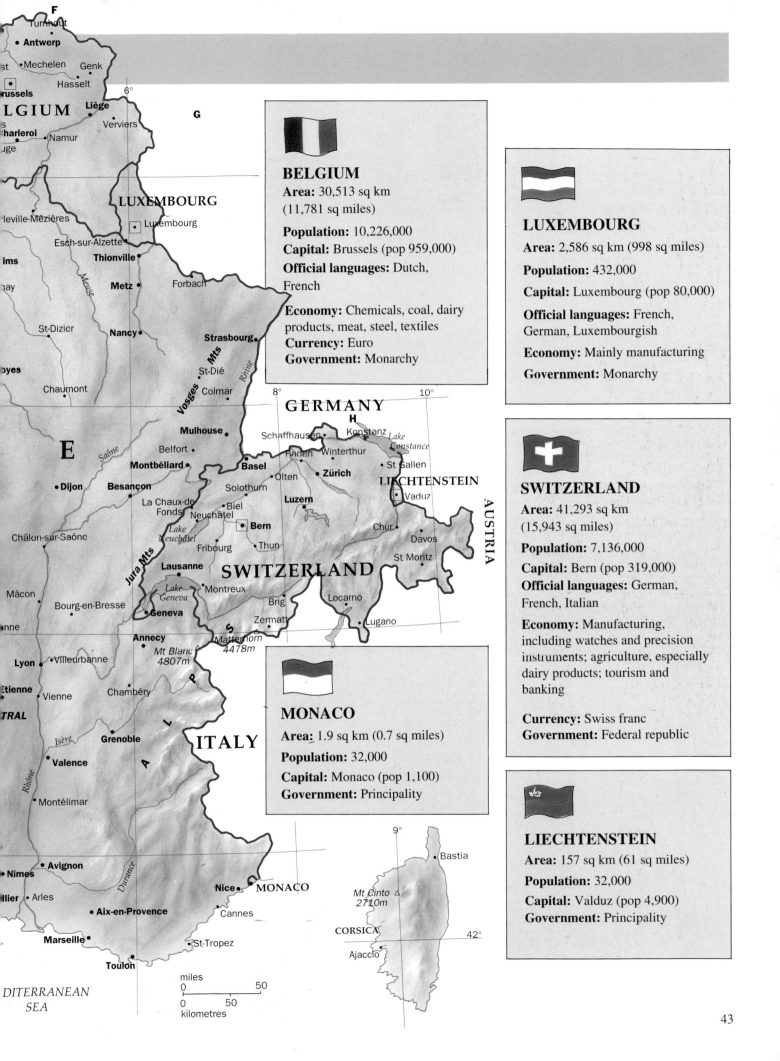

F

Turnhout
• Antwerp
• Mechelen • Genk
Hasselt
Brussels
LGIUM • Liège
Charleroi • Namur • Verviers
uge

G

LUXEMBOURG
Luxembourg
Esch-sur-Alzette
ims
Thionville
Forbach
leville-Mézières
Metz
Nancy
St-Dizier
oyes
Chaumont
Strasbourg
St-Dié
Colmar
Vosges Mts
Rhine

BELGIUM
Area: 30,513 sq km
(11,781 sq miles)
Population: 10,226,000
Capital: Brussels (pop 959,000)
Official languages: Dutch,
French
Economy: Chemicals, coal, dairy
products, meat, steel, textiles
Currency: Euro
Government: Monarchy

LUXEMBOURG
Area: 2,586 sq km (998 sq miles)
Population: 432,000
Capital: Luxembourg (pop 80,000)
Official languages: French,
German, Luxembourgish
Economy: Mainly manufacturing
Government: Monarchy

GERMANY

H

Schaffhausen Konstanz Lake
Constance
Mulhouse
Belfort
Baden Winterthur
St Gallen
E
Saône
Montbéliard **Basel**
Olten **Zürich**
LIECHTENSTEIN
Vaduz
• Dijon **Besançon**
Solothurn
La Chaux-de- Biel
Fonds Neuchâtel **Luzern**
Chur
AUSTRIA
Châlon-sur-Saône
Lake
Neuchâtel **Bern**
Davos
Fribourg Thun
St Moritz
Lausanne **SWITZERLAND**
Mâcon
Lake
Geneva Montreux
Bourg-en-Bresse Brig Locarno
Geneva Zermatt Lugano
nne
Annecy **S** Mattterhorn
4478m
Lyon • Villeurbanne Mt Blanc
4807m
Étienne • Vienne Chambéry
TRAL
Isère **Grenoble**
ITALY
Valence
Rhône
• Montélimar
• Avignon
Nîmes
Durance **Nice** **MONACO**
llier • Arles Cannes
• **Aix-en-Provence**
Marseille St-Tropez
Toulon

SWITZERLAND
Area: 41,293 sq km
(15,943 sq miles)
Population: 7,136,000
Capital: Bern (pop 319,000)
Official languages: German,
French, Italian
Economy: Manufacturing,
including watches and precision
instruments; agriculture, especially
dairy products; tourism and
banking

Currency: Swiss franc
Government: Federal republic

MONACO
Area: 1.9 sq km (0.7 sq miles)
Population: 32,000
Capital: Monaco (pop 1,100)
Government: Principality

LIECHTENSTEIN
Area: 157 sq km (61 sq miles)
Population: 32,000
Capital: Valduz (pop 4,900)
Government: Principality

Bastia
Mt Cinto
2710m
CORSICA
42°
Ajaccio

miles
0   50
0   50
kilometres

DITERRANEAN
SEA

43

UNITED KINGDOM

Area: 242,534 sq km (93,643 sq miles)

Highest point: Ben Nevis, Scotland, 1,343m (4,406ft)

Population: 59,501,000

Capital and largest city: London (pop 7,285,000)

Other cities:
Birmingham (1,013,000)
Leeds (727,000)
Glasgow (620,000)
Sheffield (531,000)

Official language: English

Religions: Protestant (53.4%), Roman Catholic (9.8%), other Christian (2.7%), Islam (2.6%), other (31.5%)

Economy: *Agriculture:* wheat, barley, potatoes, sugar beet, livestock, dairy products; *Fishing:* wet fish, shellfish; *Mining:* coal, oil and natural gas, tin, iron ore; *Industry:* machinery and transport equipment, metals, food processing, paper

Currency: Pound sterling

Government: Monarchy, whose official name is the United Kingdom of Great Britain and Northern Ireland (or U.K.). Great Britain consists of England, Scotland and Wales.

REPUBLIC OF IRELAND

Area: 70,284 sq km (27,137 sq miles)

Highest point: Carrauntoohill 1,041m (3,414ft)

Population: 3,752,000

Capital and largest city: Dublin (pop 481,000)

Official languages: Irish, English

Religions: Roman Catholic (93.1%), Church of Ireland (Protestant) (2.8%)

Main products: Machinery and transport equipment, food

Currency: Euro

Government: Republic

Countries in the U.K.

England
Area: 130,478 sq km (50,378 sq miles)
Population: 49,753,000
Capital: London (pop 7,285,000)

Northern Ireland
Area: 14,121 sq km (5,452 sq miles)
Population: 1,692,000
Capital: Belfast (pop 284,000)

Scotland
Area: 77,167 sq km (29,794 sq miles)
Population: 5,119,000
Capital: Edinburgh (pop 452,000)

Wales
Area: 20,768 sq km (8,019 sq miles)
Population: 2,937,000
Capital: Cardiff (pop 324,000)

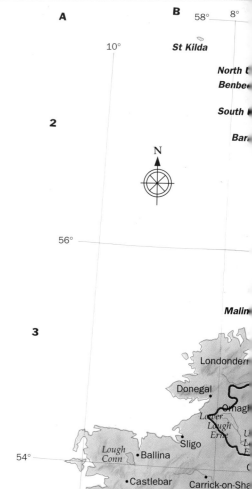

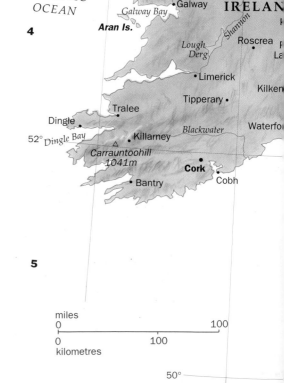

St Kilda

North U
Benbe
South
Bar

Malin

Londonder
Donegal
Omag
Lower
Lough
Erie
Sligo
Ballina
Lough
Conn
Castlebar
Carrick-on-Sha
Lough
Mask
REPUBLIC
Roscommon
Lough
Corrib
Lough
Ree
OF
Athlone
ATLANTIC
OCEAN
Galway Bay
Galway
IRELAN
Aran Is.
Shannon
Roscrea
Lough
Derg
La
Limerick
Kilken
Tipperary
Tralee
Dingle
Dingle Bay
Killarney
Blackwater
Waterfo
Carrauntoohill
1041m
Cork
Cobh
Bantry

miles
0   100
0   100
kilometres

Spain and Portugal

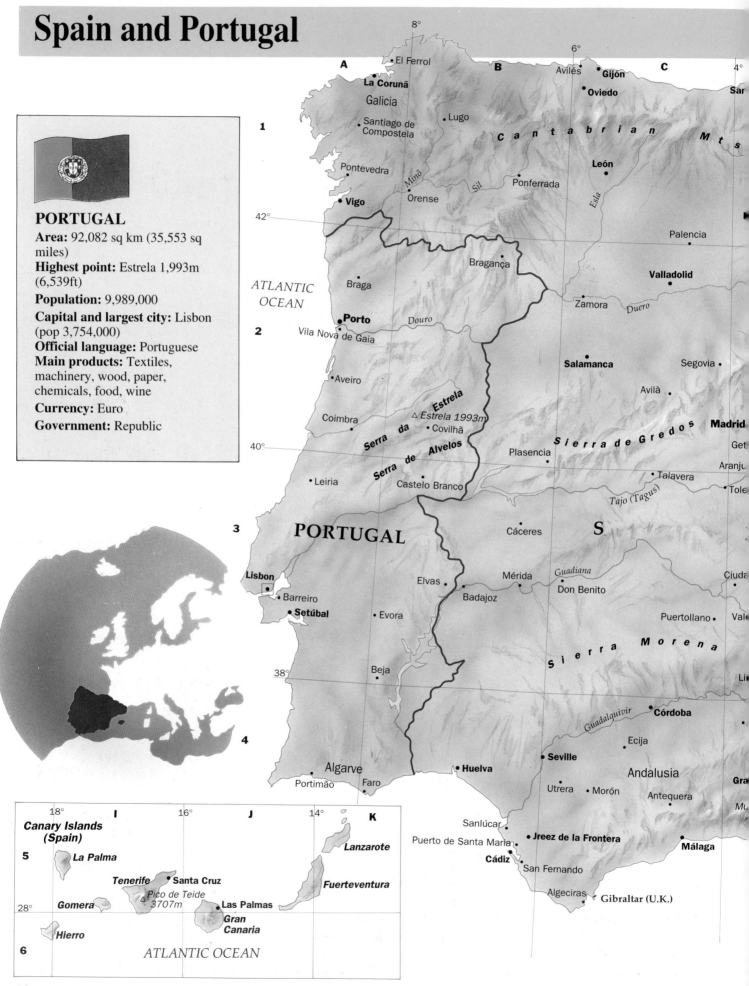

PORTUGAL

Area: 92,082 sq km (35,553 sq miles)

Highest point: Estrela 1,993m (6,539ft)

Population: 9,989,000

Capital and largest city: Lisbon (pop 3,754,000)

Official language: Portuguese

Main products: Textiles, machinery, wood, paper, chemicals, food, wine

Currency: Euro

Government: Republic

ATLANTIC OCEAN

El Ferrol
La Coruña
Galicia
Santiago de Compostela
Avilés
Gijón
Oviedo
Lugo
León
Cantabrian Mts
Pontevedra
Minõ
Sil
Ponferrada
Esla
Orense
Vigo
Palencia
Bragança
Valladolid
Braga
Zamora
Duero
Douro
Porto
Vila Nova de Gaia
Salamanca
Segovia
Aveiro
Avilá
Estrela
Estrela 1993m
Covilhã
Serra da
Serra de Alvelos
Coimbra
Sierra de Gredos
Madrid
Plasencia
Talavera
Leiria
Aranju
Castelo Branco
Tajo (Tagus)
Tole

PORTUGAL

Cáceres
S
Mérida
Guadiana
Ciuda
Elvas
Don Benito
Badajoz
Lisbon
Barreiro
Setúbal
Evora
Puertollano
Vale
Sierra Morena
Beja
Guadalquivir
Córdoba
Ecija
Seville
Andalusia
Algarve
Huelva
Gra
Portimão
Faro
Utrera
Morón
Antequera
Mu
Sanlúcar
Puerto de Santa Maria
Jreez de la Frontera
Málaga
Cádiz
San Fernando
Algeciras
Gibraltar (U.K.)

Canary Islands (Spain)

La Palma
Lanzarote
Tenerife
Santa Cruz
Fuerteventura
Gomera
Pico de Teide 3707m
Las Palmas
Hierro
Gran Canaria

ATLANTIC OCEAN

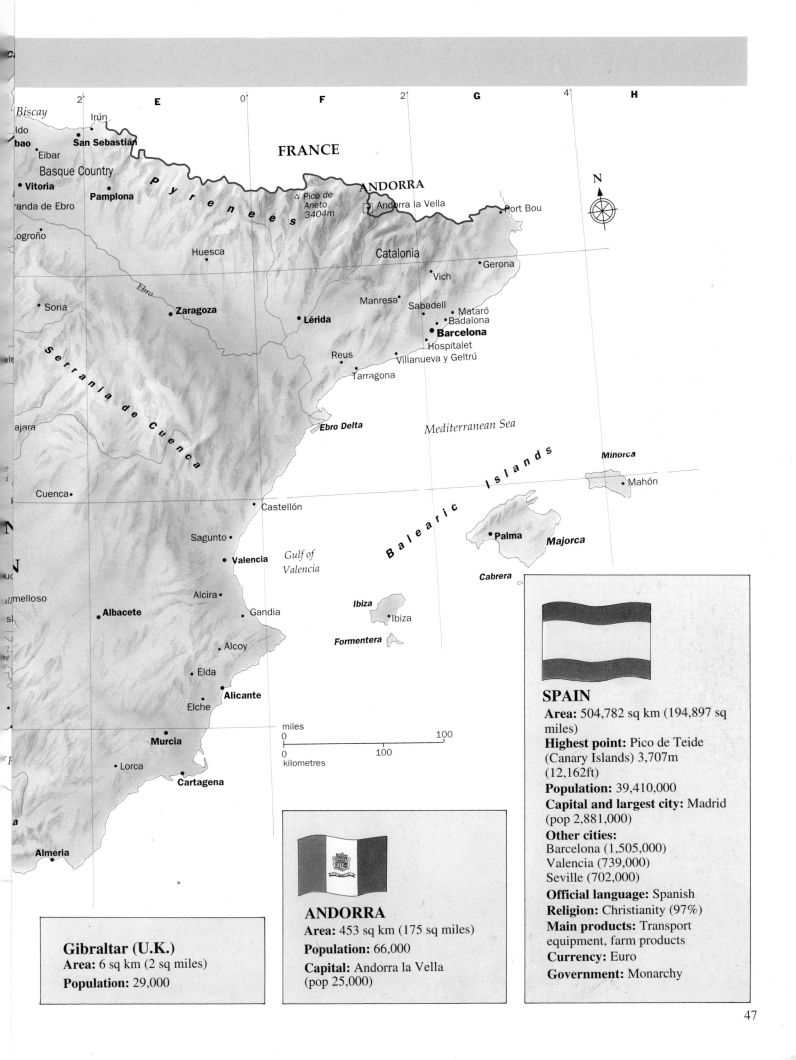

Biscay

Irún

Ido

bao • Eibar

San Sebastián

Basque Country

E

• Vitoria

Pamplona

FRANCE

ANDORRA

△ *Pico de Aneto 3404m*

□ Andorra la Vella

• Port Bou

N

anda de Ebro

ogroño

Huesca

Pyrenees

Catalonia

• Gerona

• Vich

• Soria

Ebro

Zaragoza

Lérida

Manresa•

Sabadell

• Mataró

• Badalona

• **Barcelona**

Hospitalet

Villanueva y Geltrú

ajara

Serrania de Cuenca

Reus

Tarragona

Ebro Delta

Mediterranean Sea

Balearic Islands

Minorca

• Mahón

Cuenca•

Castellón

Gulf of Valencia

• **Palma**

Majorca

Cabrera

Sagunto •

melloso

Alcira •

• **Valencia**

Ibiza

•Ibiza

sl

Albacete

• Gandia

Formentera

• Alcoy

• Elda

Alicante

Elche

Murcia

• Lorca

Cartagena

• Almeria

miles

0 — 100

0 — 100

kilometres

Gibraltar (U.K.)
Area: 6 sq km (2 sq miles)
Population: 29,000

ANDORRA
Area: 453 sq km (175 sq miles)
Population: 66,000
Capital: Andorra la Vella (pop 25,000)

SPAIN
Area: 504,782 sq km (194,897 sq miles)
Highest point: Pico de Teide (Canary Islands) 3,707m (12,162ft)
Population: 39,410,000
Capital and largest city: Madrid (pop 2,881,000)
Other cities:
Barcelona (1,505,000)
Valencia (739,000)
Seville (702,000)
Official language: Spanish
Religion: Christianity (97%)
Main products: Transport equipment, farm products
Currency: Euro
Government: Monarchy

Germany and North-Central Europe

North Sea

Baltic Sea

1

Flensburg

Frisian Islands

Kiel

• Neumunster

Stralsund

• Slupsk

Wilhelmshaven

Leeuwarden

Groningen

Bremerhaven

Lübeck

Wismar

Rostock

• Koszalin

NETHERLANDS

Oldenburg

• Bremen

Hamburg

Schwerin

Szczecin

Bydgoszc

Haarlem

Amsterdam

Enschede

Osnabrück

Hanover

Neustrelitz

Pila

52°

The Hague

Utrecht

Berlin

Inowrc

Rotterdam

Arnhem

Bielefeld

Braunschweig

Magdeburg

Potsdam

Warta

Poznan

Breda

Eindhoven

Münster

GERMANY

Saltzgitter

Halberstadt

Dessau

Oder

Neisse

BELGIUM

Duisburg

Dortmund

Kassel

Harz Mts

Halle

Cottbus

Legnica

Wroclaw

Maastricht

Krefeld

Essen

Wuppertal

Leipzig

Görlitz

Düsseldorf

Erfurt

Gera

Dresden

Kali

Aachen

Cologne

Bonn

Giessen

Thuringian Forest

Chemnitz

Usti nad

Liberec

Walbrzych

2

Koblenz

Plauen

Zwickau

Labem

Hradec Králové

Opo

Eifel

Wiesbaden

Frankfurt am Main

Ore Mts

Kladno

CZECH

Os

Mosel

Trier

Mainz

Offenbach

Schweinfurt

Main

Bamberg

Prague

Pardubice

REPUBLIC

Darmstadt

Würzburg

Plzen

Pribram

Olomouc

Mannheim

Heidelburg

Nuremburg

Jihlava

Brno

Saarbrücken

Karlsruhe

Heilbronn

Regensburg

Bohemian Forest

České

Znojmo

48°

FRANCE

Rhine

Stuttgart

Danube

Budějovice

Vah

Freiburg

Ulm

Augsburg

Krems

Vienna

Freiburg

Black Forest

Ravensburg

Munich

Inn

Linz

St. Pölten

Bratislav

3

SWITZERLAND

Lake Constance

Dornbirn

Wels

Steyr

Lake Neusiedler

Györ

Salzburg

Wiener Neustadt

Innsbruck

AUSTRIA

Leoben

Szombathely

ITALY

Alps

△ Gross Glockner 3798m

Graz

Mur

Székesfehérv

Villach

Klagenfurt

Lake Balaton

Drava

SLOVENIA

Nagykanizsa

CROATIA

NETHERLANDS

Area: 40,844 sq km (15,770 sq miles)

Population: 15,805,000

Capital: Amsterdam (pop 727,000)

Official language: Dutch

Main exports: Machinery and transport equipment, food, chemicals, mineral fuels, including natural gas, metals and metal products

Currency: Euro

Government: Monarchy

E   22°   F

N

RUSSIA   LITHUANIA

Elblag

Olsztyn

Lomza

Bialystok

oclawek

Vistula

Bug

Warsaw   • Siedlce   BELARUS

OLAND

Łódź

• Piotrków   Pulawy

Radom   • Lublin

• Kielce

testochowa   Zamość

Vistula   *San*

ce   Jaroslaw

Kraków   Rzeszów

Przemysl

rpathian Mts

▲ Gerlachovka Stit
2655m

OVAK REPUBLIC

Košice   UKRAINE

• Miskolc

Debrecen

Tisza

lapest

NGARY

kémét   Békéscsaba

Hódmezövásárhely

eged   ROMANIA

GOSLAVIA

miles
0   100
0   100
kilometres

GERMANY

Area: 356,755 sq km (137,744 sq miles)
Population: 82,100,000
Capital: Berlin (pop 3,417,000)
Other cities:
Hamburg (1,700,000)
Munich, or München (1,192,000)
Cologne, or Köln (963,000)
Frankfurt am Main (643,000)
Official language: German
Religions: Protestant (43%),
Roman Catholic (35%)
Economy: *Agriculture:* barley
wheat, rye, potatoes, sugar beet;
Fishing: cod, herring; *Mining:* coal,
lignite, iron, potash; *Industry:*
machinery and transport
equipment, motor vehicles,
chemicals and chemical products
Currency: Euro
Government: Republic

CZECH REPUBLIC

Area: 78,864 sq km (30,450 sq miles)
Population: 10,278,000
Capital: Prague (pop 1,225,000)
Currency: Czech Koruna

SLOVAK REPUBLIC

Area: 49,035 sq km (18,933 sq miles)
Population: 5,396,000
Capital: Bratislava (pop 460,000)
Currency: Slovak Koruna

POLAND

Area: 312,677 sq km (120,725 sq miles)
Population: 38,654,000
Capital: Warsaw (pop 1,632,000)
Main exports: Machinery and
transport equipment
Currency: Zloty
Government: Republic

AUSTRIA

Area: 83,849 sq km (32,374 sq miles)
Population: 8,092,000
Capital: Vienna (pop 1,608,000)
Main exports: Machinery and
transport equipment
Currency: Euro
Government: Republic

HUNGARY

Area: 93,030 sq km (35,919 sq miles)
Population: 10,068,000
Capital: Budapest (pop 1,852,000)
Main exports: Machinery and
transport equipment
Currency: Forint
Government: Republic

Italy and South-Eastern Europe

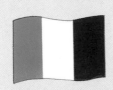

ITALY

Area: 301,225 sq km (116,304 sq miles)
Population: 57,646,000
Capital: Rome (pop 2,645,000)
Other large cities:
Milan (1,307,000)
Naples (1,020,000)
Turin (909,000)
Official language: Italian
Religion: Roman Catholic (90%)
Currency: Euro

VATICAN CITY (in Rome)

Area: 44 hectares (109 acres)
Population: 1,000

SAN MARINO

Area: 61 sq km (24 sq miles)
Population: 26,000
Capital: San Marino (pop 4,500)

SLOVENIA

Area: 20,250 sq km (7,820 sq miles)
Population: 1,986,000
Capital: Ljubljana (pop 330,000)

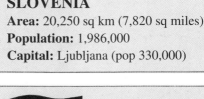

CROATIA

Area: 56,540 sq km (21,829 sq miles)
Population: 4,464,000
Capital: Zagreb (pop 1,047,000)

SERBIA & MONTENEGRO

Area: 102,169 sq km
(39,449 sq miles)
Population: 10,616,000
Capital: Belgrade (pop 1,594,000)

BOSNIA & HERCEGOVINA

Area: 51,129 sq km (19,741 sq miles)
Population: 3,881,000
Capital: Sarajevo (pop 415,000)

MALTA

Area: 316 sq km (122 sq miles)
Population: 379,000
Capital: Valletta (pop 7,000)

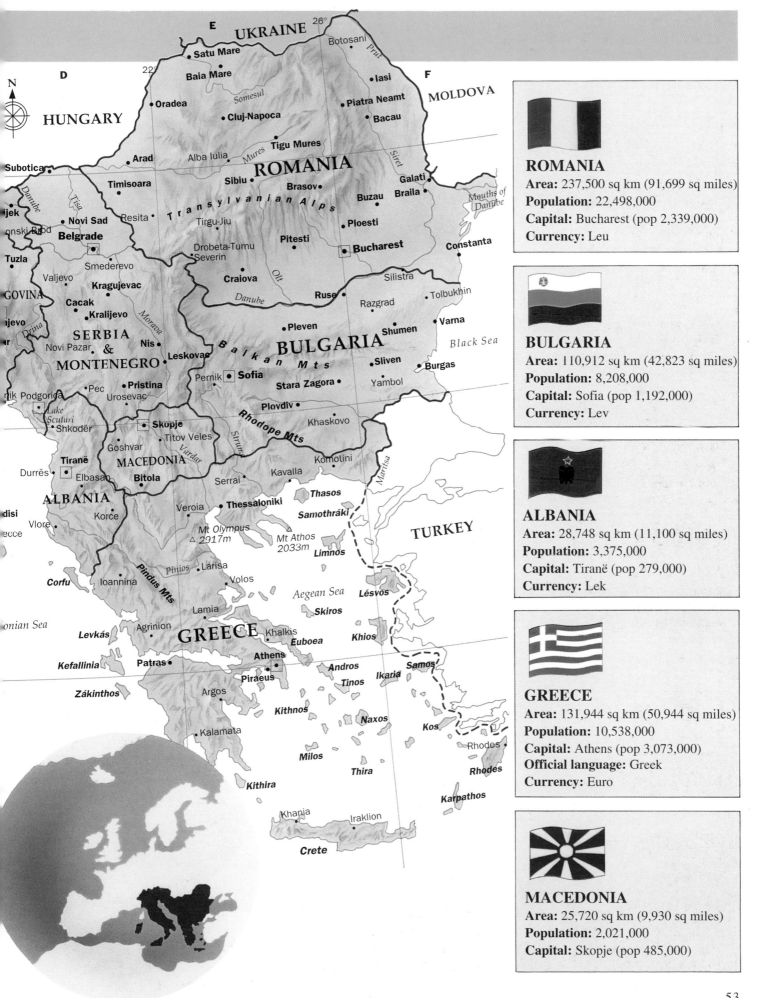

UKRAINE
E 26°
Botosani
Satu Mare
Baia Mare
Iasi
Oradea
Piatra Neamt
MOLDOVA
Cluj-Napoca
Bacau
HUNGARY
N
D
Arad
Tigu Mures
Alba Iulia
Mures
ROMANIA
Siret
Subotica
Timisoara
Sibiu
Galati
Brasov
Transylvanian Alps
Buzau
Braila
Resita
Novi Sad
Tirgu-Jiu
Mouths of
Danube
Belgrade
Ploesti
Tisa
Drobeta-Turnu
Severin
Pitesti
Bucharest
onski Brod
ijek
Tuzla
Smederevo
Constanta
Valjevo
Craiova
Olt
GOVINA
Kragujevac
Silistra
Danube
ajevo
Cacak
Ruse
Razgrad
Tolbukhin
Kraljevo
SERBIA
Novi Pazar
Nis
Pleven
Varna
&
Leskovac
Balkan Mts
BULGARIA
Shumen
MONTENEGRO
Black Sea
nik Podgorica
Pec
Pristina
Pernik
Sofia
Sliven
Burgas
Urosevac
Stara Zagora
Yambol
Lake
Scutari
Shkodër
Skopje
Plovdiv
Rhodope Mts
Khaskovo
Titov Veles
Goshvar
Vardar
Marītsa
Tiranë
MACEDONIA
Komotini
Durrës
Elbasan
Bitola
Kavalla
Serrai
ALBANIA
Veroia
Thessaloniki
Thasos
disi
Korce
Samothráki
ecce
Vlore
Mt Olympus
△ 2917m
Mt Athos
2033m
Limnos
TURKEY
Pindus Mts
Pinios
Larisa
Corfu
Ioannina
Volos
Aegean Sea
Lésvos
onian Sea
Lamia
Skiros
Levkás
Agrinion
GREECE
Khalkis
Khios
Kefallinia
Patras
Athens
Euboea
Zákinthos
Piraeus
Andros
Samos
Argos
Tinos
Ikaria
Kithnos
Naxos
Kos
Kalamata
Rhodes
Milos
Thira
Rhodes
Kithira
Karpathos
Khania
Iraklion
Crete

ROMANIA
Area: 237,500 sq km (91,699 sq miles)
Population: 22,498,000
Capital: Bucharest (pop 2,339,000)
Currency: Leu

BULGARIA
Area: 110,912 sq km (42,823 sq miles)
Population: 8,208,000
Capital: Sofia (pop 1,192,000)
Currency: Lev

ALBANIA
Area: 28,748 sq km (11,100 sq miles)
Population: 3,375,000
Capital: Tiranë (pop 279,000)
Currency: Lek

GREECE
Area: 131,944 sq km (50,944 sq miles)
Population: 10,538,000
Capital: Athens (pop 3,073,000)
Official language: Greek
Currency: Euro

MACEDONIA
Area: 25,720 sq km (9,930 sq miles)
Population: 2,021,000
Capital: Skopje (pop 485,000)

Russia and its Neighbours

RUSSIAN FEDERATION (RUSSIA)

Area: 17,075,400 sq km (6,592,849 sq miles), the world's largest country

Highest point: Mount Elbrus 5,633m (18,481ft)

Population: 146,200,000

Capital: Moscow (pop 9,310,000)

Other cities:
St Petersburg (4,800,000)
Nizhny Novgorod (1,380,000)
Novosibirsk (1,370,000)
Yekaterinburg (1,280,000)
Samara (1,260,000)

Official language: Russian

Religions: Christianity, Judaism, Islam

Main products: *Agriculture:* cotton, flax, potatoes, sugar, wheat, cattle, pigs, sheep; *Mining:* coal, copper, gold, iron ore, oil and natural gas; *Industry:* iron and steel, chemicals, machinery, paper, plastics

Currency: Rouble

Government: Federal republic

ESTONIA

Area: 45,100 sq km (17,413 sq miles)
Population: 1,442,000
Capital: Tallinn (pop 408,000)

LATVIA

Area: 64,500 sq km (24,904 sq miles)
Population: 2,431,000
Capital: Riga (pop 806,000)

LITHUANIA

Area: 65,200 sq km (25,174 sq miles)
Population: 3,699,000
Capital: Vilnius (pop 578,000)

BELARUS

Area: 207,600 sq km (80,155 sq miles)
Population: 10,038,000
Capital: Minsk (pop 1,671,000)

UKRAINE

Area: 603,700 sq km (233,090 sq miles)
Population: 49,950,000
Capital: Kyyiv (pop 2,663,000)

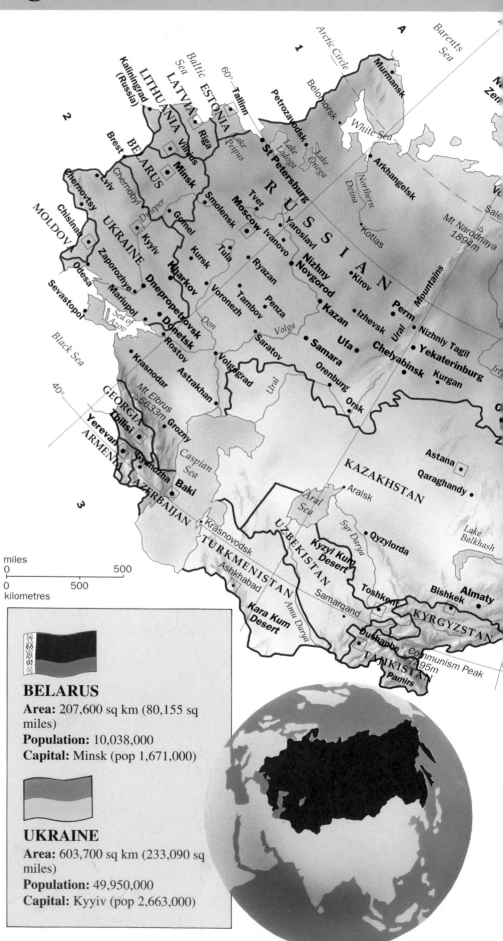

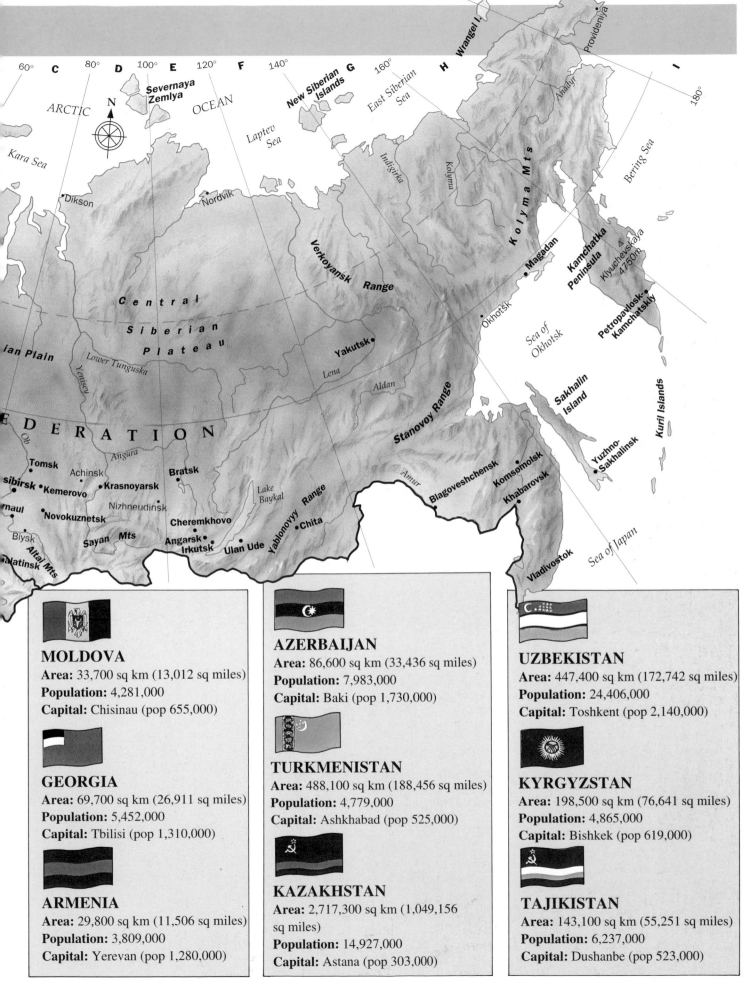

ARCTIC OCEAN

Severnaya Zemlya

Kara Sea

Laptev Sea

New Siberian Islands

East Siberian Sea

Wrangel I.

Providenlya

N

•Dikson

Nordvik

•Anadyr

Bering Sea

Verkoyansk Range

Kolyma Mts

Kolyma

Indigirka

Magadan

Kamchatka Peninsula

Klyuchevskaya 4750m

Central Siberian Plateau

ian Plain

Lower Tunguska

Yenisey

Yakutsk•

Lena

Aldan

Okhotsk•

Sea of Okhotsk

Petropavlosk-Kamchatskiy

F E D E R A T I O N

Stanovoy Range

Sakhalin Island

Kuril Islands

Ob

Angara

Tomsk•

Achinsk

Bratsk•

•Krasnoyarsk

sibirsk• •Kemerovo

Nizhneudinsk

Lake Baykal

Amur

Blagoveshchensk•

Komsomolsk•

Khabarovsk•

Yuzhno-Sakhalinsk

naul

•Novokuznetsk

Cheremkhovo•

Yablonovyy Range

•Chita

Biysk

Sayan Mts

Angarsk•

Irkutsk•

Ulan Ude•

alatinsk

Altai Mts

Vladivostok•

Sea of Japan

MOLDOVA
Area: 33,700 sq km (13,012 sq miles)
Population: 4,281,000
Capital: Chisinau (pop 655,000)

GEORGIA
Area: 69,700 sq km (26,911 sq miles)
Population: 5,452,000
Capital: Tbilisi (pop 1,310,000)

ARMENIA
Area: 29,800 sq km (11,506 sq miles)
Population: 3,809,000
Capital: Yerevan (pop 1,280,000)

AZERBAIJAN
Area: 86,600 sq km (33,436 sq miles)
Population: 7,983,000
Capital: Baki (pop 1,730,000)

TURKMENISTAN
Area: 488,100 sq km (188,456 sq miles)
Population: 4,779,000
Capital: Ashkhabad (pop 525,000)

KAZAKHSTAN
Area: 2,717,300 sq km (1,049,156 sq miles)
Population: 14,927,000
Capital: Astana (pop 303,000)

UZBEKISTAN
Area: 447,400 sq km (172,742 sq miles)
Population: 24,406,000
Capital: Toshkent (pop 2,140,000)

KYRGYZSTAN
Area: 198,500 sq km (76,641 sq miles)
Population: 4,865,000
Capital: Bishkek (pop 619,000)

TAJIKISTAN
Area: 143,100 sq km (55,251 sq miles)
Population: 6,237,000
Capital: Dushanbe (pop 523,000)

Asia

Asia is the largest continent. As well as China, Japan and India, it contains the major part of the Russian Federation, along with several other countries that were formerly part of the Soviet Union. They include Armenia, Azerbaijan and Georgia, which lie south of the Caucasus Mountains. The other countries are Kazakhstan, Kyrgyzstan, Tajikistan, Turkmenistan and Uzbekistan. These countries lie between the Caspian Sea in the west and China in the east.

China's Chang Jiang (formerly called the Yangtze Kiang) is the longest river. Mount Everest, on Nepal's border with China, is Asia's highest peak.

Asia has more than 3,500 million people, including the Asian part of Russia. It includes the world's two most populous countries, China and India, both with over a billion people.

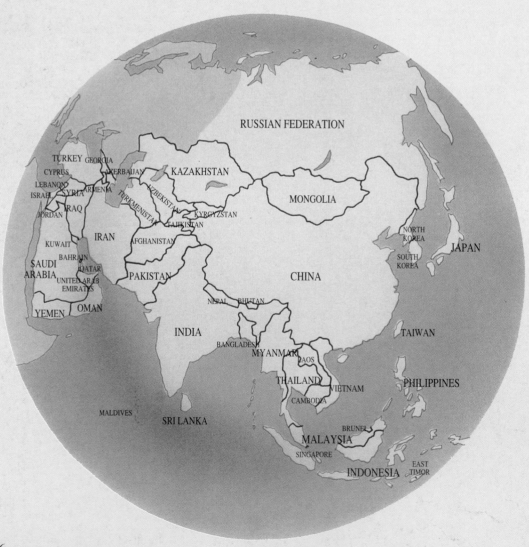

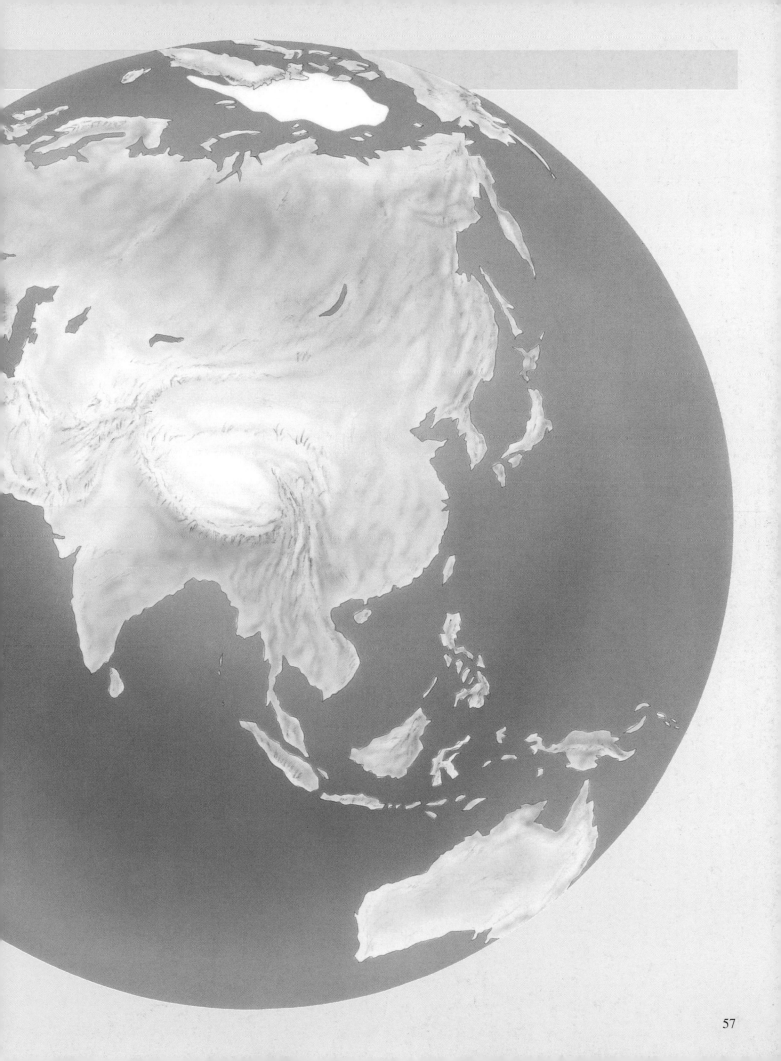

Near East

CYPRUS
Area: 9,251 sq km (3,572 sq miles)
Population: 760,000
Capital and largest city: Nicosia (pop 197,000)

ISRAEL
Area: 20,770 sq km (8,019 sq miles)
Population: 6,105,000
Capital and largest city: Jerusalem (pop 591,000)
Other large cities:
Tel Aviv-Yafo (356,000)
Haifa (252,000)
Holon (164,000)
Official languages: Hebrew, Arabic
Religions: Judaism (79.2%), Islam (14.9%), Christianity (2.1%), other including Druze (3.8%)
Currency: Shekel

TURKEY
Area: 780,576 sq km (301,382 sq miles)
Population: 64,385,000
Capital: Ankara (pop 2,984,000)
Other large cities:
Istanbul (8,260,000)
Izmir (2,081,000)
Bursa (1,066,000)
Adana (1,041,000)
Official language: Turkish
Religion: Islam (99.2%)
Currency: Turkish Lira

LEBANON
Area: 10,400 sq km (4,015 sq miles)
Population: 4,271,000
Capital and largest city: Beirut (pop 1,500,000)
Currency: Lebanese Pound

JORDAN
Area: 97,740 sq km (37,738 sq miles)
Population: 4,740,000
Capital and largest city: Amman (pop 1,378,000)
Currency: Jordanian Dinar

A   B

GREECE

Edirne   28°
Tekirdag   **Istanbul**   Bosporus
Üsküdar
Sea of Marmara   **Izmit**
40°   Gokceada I.   Dardanelles   Ada
Çanakkale   **Bursa**
Troy   Sakarya

1

N

Edremit   Balikesir   **Eskisehir**

Aegean Sea   Bergama   Kütal

Manisa   Usak
Izmir   Gediz

2

miles
0   100
0   100
kilometres

Aydin   Menderes   Lak
Egri

Denizli   Isp

36°   Finike

3

58

32° C 36° D Black Sea 40° E 44° F
Zonguldak GEORGIA
Rize
Trabzon Kars ARMENIA
Çankiri Kizil • Corum Kelkit Aras
Erzincan **Erzurum** Mt Ararat △ IRAN
5165m
Ankara **Sivas**
T U R K E Y
Lake Lake Van
Tuz **Kayseri** **Elazig** Van
Malatya K U R D I S T A N
Konya Batman
Maras **Diyarbakir** Tigris
Karaman **Urfa** Nusaybin
Tarsus **Adana** Ceyhan
Mersin Osmaniye **Gaziantep**
• Silifke Iskenderun Assad
Antakya Reservoir Euphrates
Aleppo IRAQ
CYPRUS ∴ Ebla Khabur
Nicosia Deir-ez-Zor
Famagusta **Latakia**
Larnaca **Hama** S Y R I A
Paphos **Limassol** Krak des Chevaliers ∴ Mari
Homs Palmyra
Mediterranean Sea **Tripoli**
LEBANON
Beirut Zahlé Anti-Lebanon Mts S y r i a n
Sidon **Damascus**
Tyre D e s e r t
Golan
Heights
Haifa Lake
Tiberias **Irbid**
ISRAEL • Busra
Ramat
Gan **Nablus**
Tel Aviv-Yafo West • **Zarqa**
Holon Bank **Amman**
Jerusalem
Gaza Strip Dead
Hebron Sea
Beersheba **JORDAN** **SAUDI ARABIA**
Negev
Desert
EGYPT
Petra
• Ma'an
Elat • Aqaba

SYRIA
Area: 185,180 sq km (71,498 sq miles)
Population: 15,711,000
Capital and largest city: Damascus (pop 2,270,000)
Other large cities: Aleppo (1,840,000)
Official language: Arabic
Currency: Syrian Pound

4

Arabian Peninsula and Gulf States

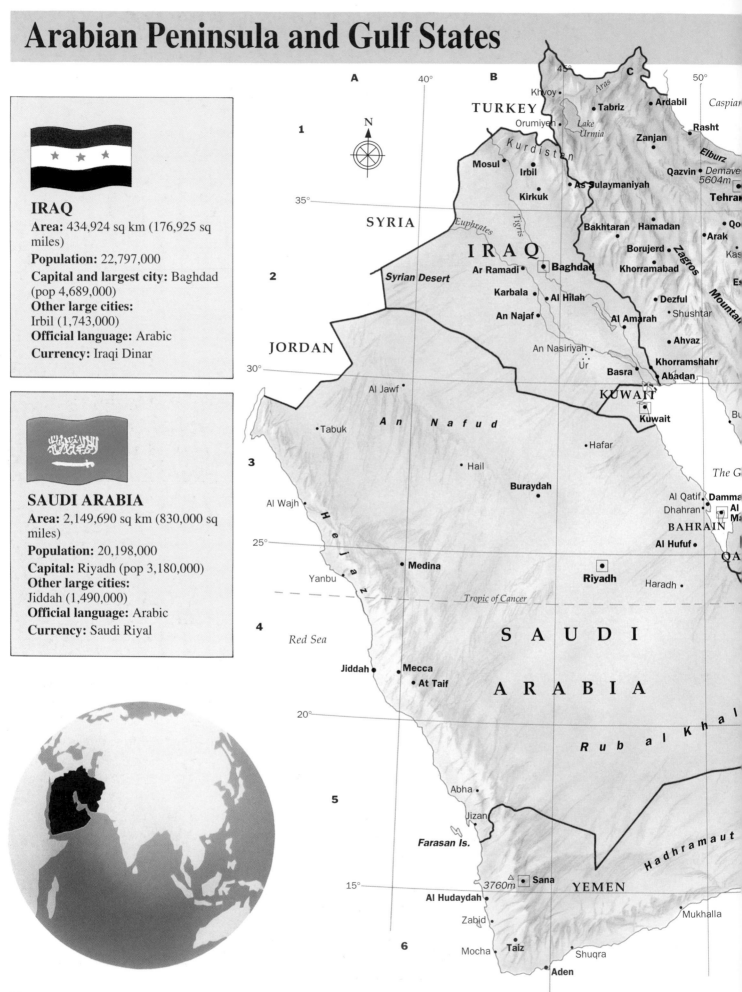

IRAQ

Area: 434,924 sq km (176,925 sq miles)

Population: 22,797,000

Capital and largest city: Baghdad (pop 4,689,000)

Other large cities:
Irbil (1,743,000)

Official language: Arabic

Currency: Iraqi Dinar

SAUDI ARABIA

Area: 2,149,690 sq km (830,000 sq miles)

Population: 20,198,000

Capital: Riyadh (pop 3,180,000)

Other large cities:
Jiddah (1,490,000)

Official language: Arabic

Currency: Saudi Riyal

TURKMENISTAN

55° E 60° F

Gorgan

Neyshabur • **Mashhad**

sht-e Kavir

AFGHANISTAN

Dasht-e-Lut

Birjand

• Yazd

RAN

• **Kerman**

Zahedan

• Bam

PAKISTAN

Bandar Abbas

Strait of Hormuz

Chah Bahar

Sharjah
Dubai

Gulf of Oman

ED

AB EMIRATES

abi

Al Khaburah

□ Muscat

△
3035m

OMAN

Al Masira

h u f a r

Salalah

Kuria Muria I.

Arabian Sea

miles
0 200

0 200
kilometres

IRAN
Area: 1,648,000 sq km (636,296 sq miles)
Population: 62,977,000
Capital and largest city: Tehran (pop 6,758,000)
Other large cities:
Mashad (1,887,000)
Esfahan (1,266,000)
Official language: Farsi (Persian)
Currency: Iranian Rial

KUWAIT
Area: 17,818 sq km (6,880 sq miles)
Population: 1,924,000
Capital: Kuwait (pop 28,000)
Currency: Kuwaiti Dinar

YEMEN
Area: 527,968 sq km (203,850 sq miles)
Population: 17,048,000
Capital and largest city: Sana (pop 1,231,000)
Other large cities: Aden (562,000)
Currency: Yemen Rial

BAHRAIN
Area: 622 sq km (240 sq miles)
Population: 666,000
Capital: Al Manamah (pop 162,000)

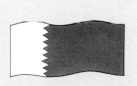

QATAR
Area: 11,000 sq km (4,247 sq miles)
Population: 565,000
Capital and largest city: Doha (pop 391,000)

UNITED ARAB EMIRATES
Area: 83,600 sq km (32,278 sq miles)
Population: 2,815,000
Capital: Abu Dhabi (pop 904,000)

OMAN
Area: 212,457 sq km (82,030 sq miles)
Population: 2,348,000
Capital and largest city: Muscat (pop 635,000)
Religions: Islam (86%), Hinduism (13%)
Currency: Omani Rial

India and Southern Asia

AFGHANISTAN
Area: 647,497 sq km (250,000 sq miles)
Population: 25,869,000
Capital and largest city: Kabul (pop 2,450,000)
Religion: Islam (99%)
Currency: Afghani

INDIA
Area: 3,287,590 sq km (1,269,346 sq miles)
Highest point: Kanchenjunga, on border with Nepal, 8,598m (28,208ft)
Population: 1,015,923,000
Capital: New Delhi (pop 301,000)
Other large cities:
Mumbai (12,596,000)
Kolkata (11,022,000)
Delhi (8,419,000)
Chennai (5,422,000)
Hyderabad (4,253,000)
Bangalore (4,130,000)
Official languages: Hindi, English
Religions: Hinduism (82.6%), Islam (11.4%), Christianity (2.4%), Sikhism (2%), other religions (1.6%)
Economy: *Agriculture:* rice and other grains, pulses, cotton, sugar cane; *Fishing:* sea fishing; *Mining:* coal, iron ore, manganese; *Industry:* textiles, food products, steel, machinery, transport equipment
Currency: Indian Rupee
Government: Federal republic

PAKISTAN
Area: 796,095 sq km (307,374 sq miles)
Population: 134,790,000
Capital: Islamabad (pop 191,000)
Other large cities:
Karachi (9,269,000)
Lahore (5,063,000)
Official language: Urdu
Religion: Islam (96.7%)
Main products: Rice, cotton, textiles
Currency: Pakistan Rupee

NEPAL
Area: 140,797 sq km (54,362 sq miles)
Highest point: Mount Everest, on the border with China, 8,848m (29,028ft)
Population: 23,384,000
Capital and largest city: Katmandu (pop 533,000)
Official language: Nepali
Currency: Nepali Rupee

Map labels: TURKMENISTAN, Mazar-i-Sharif, Baghlar, Herat, Hindu, Kus, Kabul, Ja, Ghazni, AFGHANISTAN, Farah, IRAN, Kandahar, Rigestan Desert, Quetta, Kalat, PAKISTAN, Sulaim, Baluchistan Plateau, Sukkur, Indus, Gwadar, Nawabsha, Hyderabad, Karachi, Tropic of Cancer, Jamnagar, Ra, Bha, Arabian Sea, IND

65° 35° 30° 25° 20° 15° 10°
A B 1 2 3 4 5 6 7

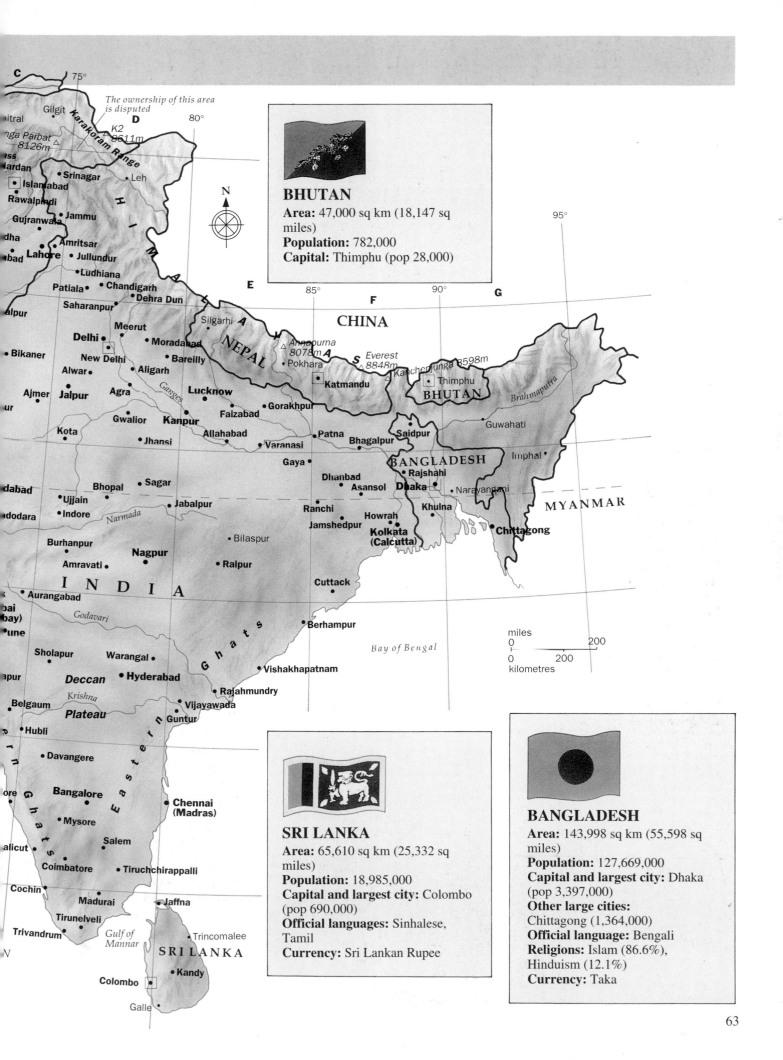

BHUTAN
Area: 47,000 sq km (18,147 sq miles)
Population: 782,000
Capital: Thimphu (pop 28,000)

SRI LANKA
Area: 65,610 sq km (25,332 sq miles)
Population: 18,985,000
Capital and largest city: Colombo (pop 690,000)
Official languages: Sinhalese, Tamil
Currency: Sri Lankan Rupee

BANGLADESH
Area: 143,998 sq km (55,598 sq miles)
Population: 127,669,000
Capital and largest city: Dhaka (pop 3,397,000)
Other large cities: Chittagong (1,364,000)
Official language: Bengali
Religions: Islam (86.6%), Hinduism (12.1%)
Currency: Taka

63

China, Japan and the Far East

KAZAKHSTAN

KYRGYZSTAN

TAJIKISTAN

PAKISTAN

INDIA

NEPAL

Tian Shan

Kashi

Shache

Taklimakan Desert

Kunlun Mountains

Tibetan Plateau

Himalayas

Xigaze

Lhasa

Everest 8848m

BHUTAN

Yining

Urumqi

Altun Mts

Lake Uvs

Altai Mts

Gobi Desert

Lake Hovsgol

Darhan

Erdenet

Ulan Bator

MONGOLIA

Yumen

Qilian Mountains

Lake Qinghai

Xining

Huang He

Great Wall

Lanzhou

Yinchuan

Mu Us Deser

Baoji

Xi'a

CHINA

Chengdu

Nanchong

Chang Jiang (Yangtze Riv)

Zigong

Luzhou

Zunyi

Giuyang

Chongqing

Sha

Kunming

Yunnan Plateau

Gejiu

Xi Jiang

G

Lu

W

Nanni

MYANMAR

LAOS

VIETNAM

Zhanjian

Hair

Salween

Mekong

108

CHINA
Area: 9,596,961 sq km (3,705,408) sq miles)

Highest point: Mount Everest, on the border with Nepal, 8,848m (29,028ft)

Longest river: Chang Jiang (formerly Yangtze Kiang), 5,530km (3,436 miles)

Population: 1,231,629,000

Capital: Beijing (pop 10,820,000)

Other large cities:
Shanghai (12,910,000)
Tianjin (8,970,000)
Shenyang (4,740,000)
Wuhan (4,450,000)

Official language: Mandarin Chinese

Religions: Confucianism, Buddhism, Taoism, Islam

Economy: *Agriculture:* rice, wheat, oilseed, cotton; *Fishing:* fresh and sea fishing; *Mining:* coal, iron, oil; *Industry:* iron and steel, machinery, textiles

Currency: Yuan

Government: People's Republic

MONGOLIA
Area: 1,565,000 sq km (604,250 sq miles)

Population: 2,378,000

Capital and largest city: Ulan Bator (pop 744,000)

Official language: Mongolian

Religions: Tantric Buddhism, Islam

Currency: Tugrik

120°

E
132°
F
144°

RUSSIA

Greater Hinggan Range
Lesser Hinggan Range
Amur

• Qiqihar
Jixi
• Harbin
Baicheng
Manchurian Plain
• Mudanjiang
• Jilin
Changchun •
Siping
• Chongjin
Shenyang
Fuxin • Fushun
• Benxi
Jinzhou • Anshan
• Sinuiju
Hamhung
NORTH KOREA
• Wonsan
Yingkou

Beijing
• Tangshan
Pyongyang •
Nampo
□ Seoul
Tianjin •
Dalian
Shijiazhuang
Yantai
• Inchon
SOUTH KOREA
• Taejon
Bo Hai Sea
• Taegu
Xingtai
Zibo
• Weifang
• Ulsan
• Pusan
Jinan
• Qingdao
Kwangju •
Hiroshima
Yellow Sea
• Cheju
Kaifeng
Lianyungang
Kitakyushu
Fukuoka
Xuzhou
Nagasaki
Kumamoto
Huainan
Nanjing
Nantong
Kagoshima
Kyushu
Hefei •
Wuxi
Shanghai
East China Sea
Wuhu
Suzhou
Hangzhou •
Anqing
• Ningbo
• Jingdezhen
Nanchang
• Wenzhou
Ryukyu Islands
• Naha

Sea of Japan

Asahikawa
Sapporo
Hokkaido
Hakodate
Aomori
• Morioka
Akita
• Sendai
Niigata
Honshu
JAPAN
Kanazawa
Tokyo
Kawasaki
• Chiba
Mt Fuji
Yokohama
Kyoto
3776m
Nagoya
Kobe
Osaka
Okayama
Sakai
Matsuyama
Shikoku

PACIFIC OCEAN

• Fuzhou
Chilung
Taipei □
Xiamen
Taichung
Shantou
Tainan
TAIWAN
• Hong Kong
Gaoxiong

Tropic of Cancer

South China Sea

miles
0   500
0   500
kilometres

JAPAN
Area: 377,708 sq km (145,800 sq miles)
Highest point: Mount Fuji 3,776m (12,388ft)
Population: 126,570,000
Capital: Tokyo (pop 7,885,000)
Other large cities:
Yokohama (3,352,000)
Osaka (2,472,000)
Official language: Japanese
Religions: Shintoism (39.5%), Buddhism (38.3%)
Main products: Manufactures, including machinery, vehicles, electronic goods, instruments
Currency: Yen
Government: Monarchy

NORTH KOREA
Area: 120,538 sq km (46,540 sq miles)
Population: 23,414,000
Capital and largest city: Pyongyang (pop 3,136,000)

SOUTH KOREA
Area: 98,484 sq km (38,025 sq miles)
Population: 46,858,000
Capital and largest city: Seoul (pop 10,231,000)

TAIWAN
Area: 36,000 sq km (13,900 sq miles)
Population: 21,966,000
Capital and largest city: Taipei (pop 2,640,000)

65

South-Eastern Asia

THAILAND
Area: 514,000 sq km (198,457 sq miles)
Population: 60,246,000
Capital and largest city: Bangkok (pop 6,320,000)
Official language: Thai
Currency: Baht

MALAYSIA
Area: 329,749 sq km (127,317 sq miles)
Population: 22,710,000
Capital and largest city: Kuala Lumpur (pop 1,145,000)
Official language: Malay
Currency: Ringgit (Malaysian Dollar)

SINGAPORE
Area: 581 sq km (224 sq miles)
Population: 3,952,000
Capital and largest city: Singapore
Official languages: Chinese, Malay, Tamil, English
Currency: Singapore Dollar

LAOS
Area: 236,800 sq km (91,429 sq miles)
Population: 5,097,000
Capital and largest city: Vientiane (pop 377,000)

MYANMAR (Burma)
Area: 676,552 sq km (261,218 sq miles)
Population: 45,029,000
Capital and largest city: Yangon (formerly Rangoon, pop 4,101,000)
Official language: Burmese
Currency: Kyat

INDIA

BANGLADESH

MYANMAR (Burma)

Myitkyina

CHINA

Tropic of Cancer

Mandalay

Akyab

Meiktila

Red

Hanoi

LAOS

VIETN

Chiang Mai

Luang Prabang

Vinh

Bassein

Pegu

Vientiane

Yangon

Phitsanulok

Udon Thani

Annam

THAILAND

Moulmein

Khon Kaen

Nakhon Sawan

Ubon Ratchathani

Pakse

Da

Nakhon Ratchasima

Bangkok

Sisophon

Batambang

Lake Tonle Sap

Kratie

Mergui

Chon Buri

CAMBODIA

Phnom Penh

Ho Chi Mi

Rach Gia

My

Can Tho

Phuket

Nakhon Si Thammarat

Hat Yai

Songkhla

Banda Aceh

Kota Baharu

Andaman Sea

INDIAN OCEAN

George Town

Ipoh

M A L A

Medan

Pematangsiantar

Kuala Lumpur

Simeulue

Lake Toba

Kelang

Nias

Sumatra

Johor Baharu

Singapore

Pakanbaru

Padang

Por

Siberut

Kerintji 3805m

Jambi

I N D

Bangka

Barisan Range

Palembang

Tanjungkarang

Jakar

Bogor

Sukabumi

B

Mentawai Islands

Equator

miles
0   500
0   500
kilometres

66

VIETNAM
Area: 329,556 sq km (127,242 sq miles)
Population: 77,515,000
Capital city: Hanoi (pop 1,089,000)
Currency: Dong

BRUNEI
Area: 5,765 sq km (2,226 sq miles)
Population: 322,000
Capital and largest city: Bandar Seri Begawan (pop 85,000)

CAMBODIA
Area: 181,035 sq km (69,898 sq miles)
Population: 11,757,000
Capital and largest city: Phnom Penh (pop 938,000)
Currency: Riel

PHILIPPINES
Area: 300,000 sq km (115,831 sq miles)
Population: 74,259,000
Capital and largest city: Manila (pop 1,673,000)
Currency: Philippine Peso

INDONESIA
Area: 1,889,960 sq km (729,718 sq miles)
Population: 206,102,000
Capital and largest city: Jakarta (pop 8,259,000)
Currency: Rupiah

EAST TIMOR
Area: 14,609 sq km (5,641 sq miles)
Population: 920,000
Capital: Dili (pop 60,000)

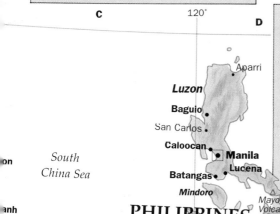

South China Sea

Luzon

Aparri

Baguio

San Carlos

Caloocan

Manila

Batangas

Lucena

Mindoro

Mayon Volcano 2421m

PHILIPPINES

Samar

Panay

Iloilo · Cadiz · **Leyte**

Bacolod · Cebu

Palawan

Negros · **Bohol**

Sulu Sea

Butuan

Iligan · Cagayan de Oro

Zamboanga

Mindanao

Basilan

Mt Apo 2954m △ · Davao

General Santos

PACIFIC OCEAN

Talaud Is.

dar Seri Begawan

BRUNEI

Sabah

Tawau

Celebes Sea

Sangihe Is.

Sarawak

Manado

Halmahera

Borneo

Waigeo

Manokwari

Sarmi

Samarinda

Sulawesi (Celebes)

Palu

Obi

Misool

Balikpapan

New Guinea

alimantan

Sula Is.

Ceram Sea

Maoke △ Range

E **S** **I** **A**

Banjarmasin

Majene

Kendari

Buru

Ceram

Fakfak

Ambon

Puncak Jaya 5030m

PAPUA NEW GUINEA

Java Sea

Ujung Pandang

Banda Sea

West Papua

ang

Aru Is.

Surabaya

karta · Malang · **Bali**

Flores Sea

Wetar

Tanimbar Is.

Merauke

Lombok · Sumbawa

Flores

Dili

East Timor

Sumba

Timor

Africa

Africa is the world's second largest continent. Much of the land is wilderness. Areas with few people include the Sahara in North Africa, the world's biggest desert, and the Kalahari and Namib deserts in southern Africa. Africa has dense forests around the Equator, together with huge grasslands, the home of many wild animals.

The continent's rivers include the world's longest, the Nile. The highest mountain is Kilimanjaro, an old volcano in Tanzania.

Africa contains 53 independent countries, with a total population of more than 770 million. A few countries are rich in minerals and some have industries, but more than half of the people of Africa are poor farmers.

North Africa

ALGERIA
Area: 2,381,741 sq km (919,595 sq miles)
Population: 29,950,000
Capital: Algiers (pop 1,519,000)

TUNISIA
Area: 163,610 sq km (63,170 sq miles)
Population: 9,457,000
Capital: Tunis (pop 1,860,000)

MAURITANIA
Area: 1,030,700 sq km (397,956 sq miles)
Population: 2,598,000
Capital: Nouakchott (pop 881,000)

MOROCCO
Area: 446,550 sq km (172,414 sq miles)
Population: 28,238,000
Capital: Rabat (pop 1,293,000)

WESTERN SAHARA
(occupied by Morocco)
Area: 266,000 sq km (102,703 sq miles)
Population: 250,000

MALI
Area: 1,240,000 sq km (478,767 sq miles)
Population: 10,584,000
Capital: Bamako (pop 1,083,000)

NIGER
Area: 1,267,000 sq km (489,191 sq miles)
Population: 10,496,000
Capital: Niamey (pop 392,000)

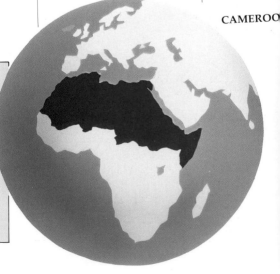

LIBYA
Area: 1,759,000 sq km (679,362 sq miles)
Population: 5,419,000
Capital: Tripoli (pop 1,773,000)

CHAD
Area: 1,284,000 sq km (495,755 sq miles)
Population: 7,486,000
Capital: N'Djamena (pop 998,000)

EGYPT
Area: 1,001,449 sq km (386,662 sq miles)
Population: 62,655,000
Capital: Cairo (pop 7,109,000)

ETHIOPIA
Area: 1,128,220 sq km (435,608 sq miles)
Population: 62,782,000
Capital: Addis Ababa (pop 2,534,000)

DJIBOUTI
Area: 22,000 sq km (8,494 sq miles)
Population: 648,000
Capital: Djibouti (pop 523,000)

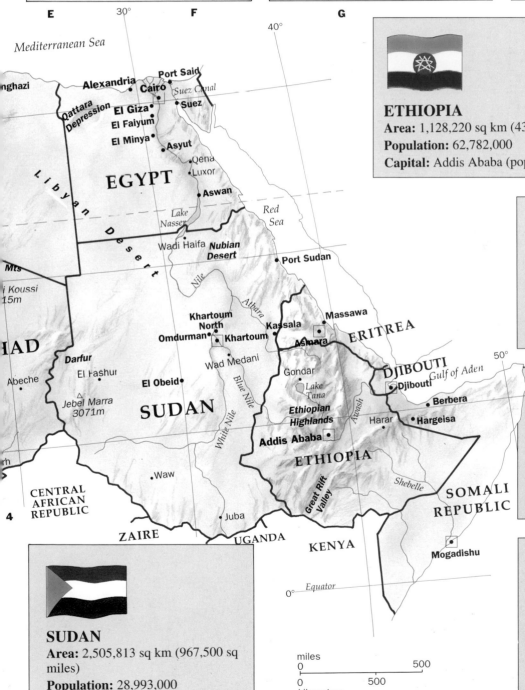

ERITREA
Area: 93,680 sq km (36,170 sq miles)
Population: 3,991,000
Capital: Asmara (pop 400,000)

SUDAN
Area: 2,505,813 sq km (967,500 sq miles)
Population: 28,993,000
Capital: Khartoum (pop 2,628,000)

SOMALI REPUBLIC
Area: 637,657 sq km (246,201 sq miles)
Population: 9,388,000
Capital: Mogadishu (pop 1,162,000)

71

West Africa

Cape Verde Islands

Santa Antão

Sal I.

Boa Vista I.

Sào Tiago I.

Brava

Praia

1

2

A   B

21°   16°

CAPE VERDE
Area: 4,033 sq km (1,557 sq miles)
Population: 428,000
Capital: Praia (pop 76,000)

GAMBIA
Area: 11,295 sq km (4,361 sq miles)
Population: 1,251,000
Capital: Banjul (pop 229,000)

GUINEA-BISSAU
Area: 36,125 sq km (13,948 sq miles)
Population: 1,185,000
Capital: Bissau (pop 197,000)

GUINEA
Area: 245,857 sq km (94,926 sq miles)
Population: 7,251,000
Capital: Conakry (pop 1,320,000)

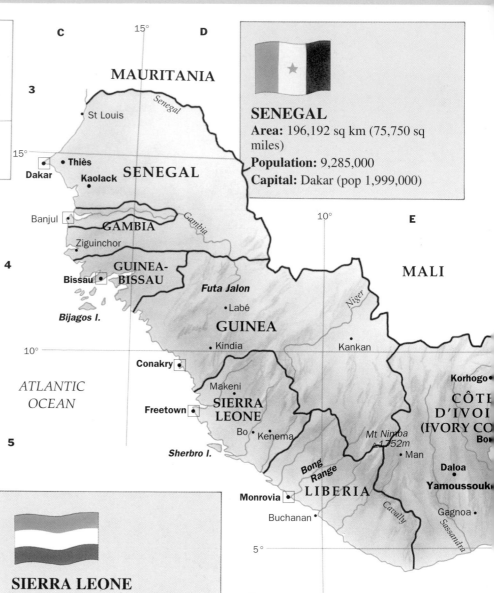

C   15°   D

3

MAURITANIA

St Louis

Senegal

15°

Thiès   SENEGAL

Dakar

Kaolack

Banjul

GAMBIA

Ziguinchor   Gambia

GUINEA-BISSAU

Bissau

Futa Jalon

Labé

Bijagos I.

10°

GUINEA

Kindia

ATLANTIC
OCEAN

Conakry

Makeni

Freetown

SIERRA
LEONE

Bo   Kenema

Sherbro I.

Monrovia   LIBERIA

Buchanan

SENEGAL (flag)

SENEGAL
Area: 196,192 sq km (75,750 sq miles)
Population: 9,285,000
Capital: Dakar (pop 1,999,000)

10°   E

MALI

Niger

Kankan

Korhogo

CÔTE
D'IVOI
(IVORY CO

Bo

Mt Nimba
1752m

Man

Daloa

Yamoussouk

Gagnoa

Cavally

Sassandra

5°

4

5

6

SIERRA LEONE
Area: 71,740 sq km (27,699 sq miles)
Population: 4,949,000
Capital: Freetown (pop 470,000)

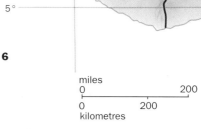

LIBERIA
Area: 111,369 sq km (43,000 sq miles)
Population: 3,044,000
Capital: Monrovia (pop 479,000)

miles
0   200
0   200
kilometres

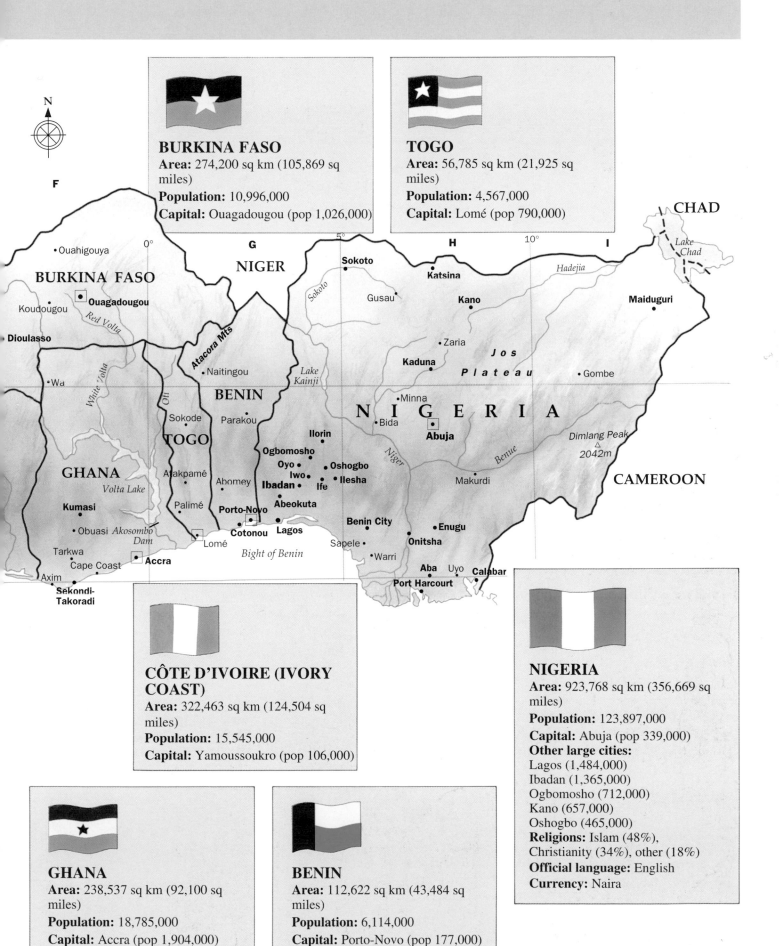

BURKINA FASO
Area: 274,200 sq km (105,869 sq miles)
Population: 10,996,000
Capital: Ouagadougou (pop 1,026,000)

TOGO
Area: 56,785 sq km (21,925 sq miles)
Population: 4,567,000
Capital: Lomé (pop 790,000)

CÔTE D'IVOIRE (IVORY COAST)
Area: 322,463 sq km (124,504 sq miles)
Population: 15,545,000
Capital: Yamoussoukro (pop 106,000)

NIGERIA
Area: 923,768 sq km (356,669 sq miles)
Population: 123,897,000
Capital: Abuja (pop 339,000)
Other large cities:
Lagos (1,484,000)
Ibadan (1,365,000)
Ogbomosho (712,000)
Kano (657,000)
Oshogbo (465,000)
Religions: Islam (48%), Christianity (34%), other (18%)
Official language: English
Currency: Naira

GHANA
Area: 238,537 sq km (92,100 sq miles)
Population: 18,785,000
Capital: Accra (pop 1,904,000)

BENIN
Area: 112,622 sq km (43,484 sq miles)
Population: 6,114,000
Capital: Porto-Novo (pop 177,000)

Central Africa

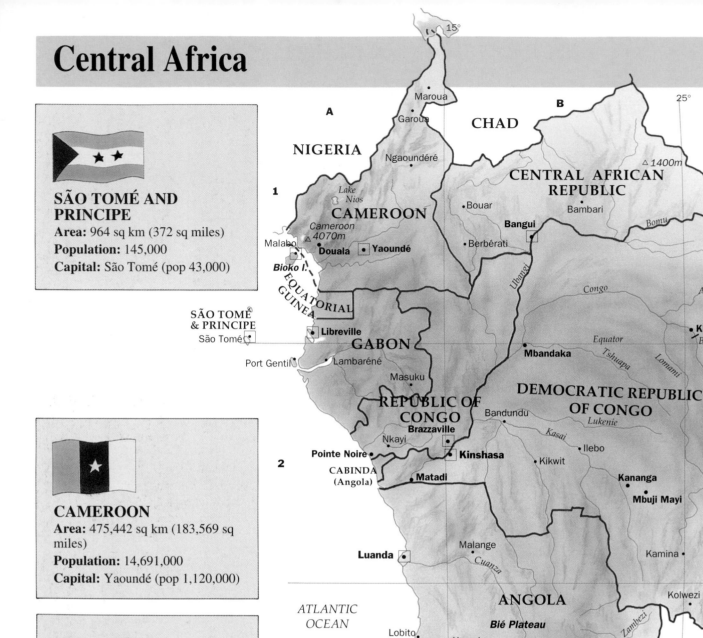

SÃO TOMÉ AND PRINCIPE
Area: 964 sq km (372 sq miles)
Population: 145,000
Capital: São Tomé (pop 43,000)

CAMEROON
Area: 475,442 sq km (183,569 sq miles)
Population: 14,691,000
Capital: Yaoundé (pop 1,120,000)

EQUATORIAL GUINEA
Area: 28,051 sq km (10,831 sq miles)
Population: 443,000
Capital: Malabo (pop 30,000)

GABON
Area: 267,667 sq km (103,347 sq miles)
Population: 1,208,000
Capital: Libreville (pop 523,000)

REPUBLIC OF CONGO
Area: 342,000 sq km (132,047 sq miles)
Population: 2,859,000
Capital: Brazzaville (pop 937,000)

ANGOLA
Area: 1,246,700 sq km (481,354 sq miles)
Population: 12,357,000
Capital: Luanda (pop 2,550,000)

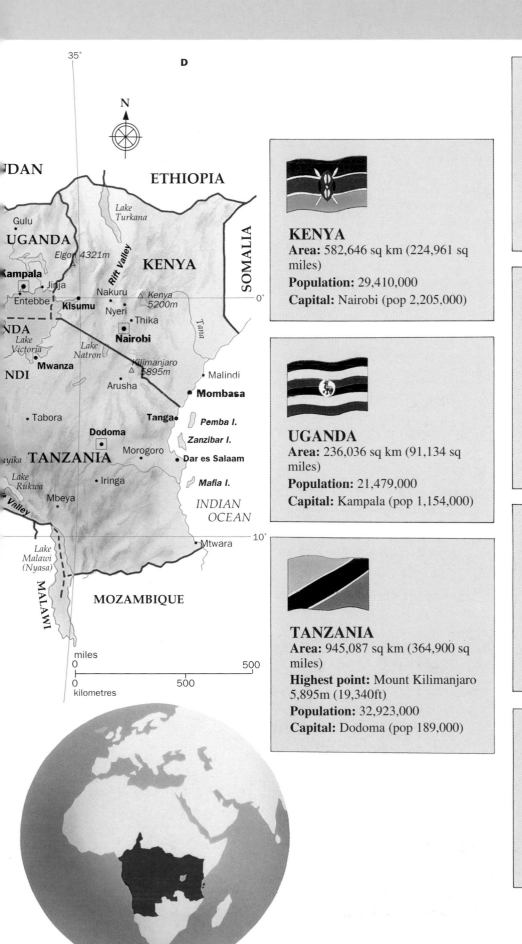

SUDAN
ETHIOPIA
UGANDA
Gulu
Lake Turkana
Elgon 4321m
Kampala
Jinja
KENYA
Entebbe
Kisumu
Nakuru
Nyeri
Thika
Rift Valley
△ *Kenya 5200m*
0°
SOMALIA
Tana
Nairobi
Lake Victoria
Lake Natron
Mwanza
Kilimanjaro
5895m
Arusha
Malindi
Tabora
Mombasa
Dodoma
Tanga
Pemba I.
Zanzibar I.
Morogoro
Dar es Salaam
TANZANIA
Mafia I.
Iringa
INDIAN
OCEAN
Lake Rukwa
10°
Mbeya
Mtwara
Lake Malawi (Nyasa)
MALAWI
MOZAMBIQUE

miles
0   500
0   500
kilometres

KENYA
Area: 582,646 sq km (224,961 sq miles)
Population: 29,410,000
Capital: Nairobi (pop 2,205,000)

UGANDA
Area: 236,036 sq km (91,134 sq miles)
Population: 21,479,000
Capital: Kampala (pop 1,154,000)

TANZANIA
Area: 945,087 sq km (364,900 sq miles)
Highest point: Mount Kilimanjaro 5,895m (19,340ft)
Population: 32,923,000
Capital: Dodoma (pop 189,000)

CENTRAL AFRICAN REPUBLIC
Area: 622,984 sq km (240,535 sq miles)
Population: 3,540,000
Capital: Bangui (pop 622,000)

DEMOCRATIC REPUBLIC OF CONGO
Area: 2,345,409 sq km (905,568 sq miles)
Population: 49,776,000
Capital: Kinshasa (pop 4,885,000)
Official language: French
Currency: Zaire

RWANDA
Area: 26,338 sq km (10,169 sq miles)
Population: 8,310,000
Capital: Kigali (pop 369,000)

BURUNDI
Area: 27,834 sq km (10,747 sq miles)
Population: 6,678,000
Capital: Bujumbura (pop 321,000)

Southern Africa

ZAMBIA
Area: 752,614 sq km (290,586 sq miles)
Population: 9,881,000
Capital: Lusaka (pop 1,577,000)

MALAWI
Area: 118,484 sq km (45,747 sq miles)
Population: 10,788,000
Capital: Lilongwe (pop 1,000,000)

NAMIBIA
Area: 824,292 sq km (318,261 sq miles)
Population: 1,701,000
Capital: Windhoek (pop 202,000)

DEMOCRATIC REPUBLIC OF CONGO

TANZANIA

Lake Mweru
Lake Tanganyika
Lake Bangweulu
Kasama
Muchinga Mts
Ruvuma
Lake Malawi (Nyasa)

Mufulira
Chingola
Kitwe
Ndola
Luangwa
MALAWI
Lichinga

ZAMBIA
Kabwe
Lilongwe

ANGOLA

Lusaka
Kafue
Cabora Bassa Dam
Shire
Nampula
Moçamb

Zambezi
Kariba Dam
Tete
Blantyre

Okavango
Rundu
Caprivi Strip
Livingstone
Lake Kariba
MOZAMBIQUE

Etosha Pan
Tsumeb

NAMIBIA

Windhoek

Victoria Falls
ZIMBABWE
Harare
Mutare
Quelimane

Okavango Basin
Kwekwe
Gweru
Chimoio

Masvingo
Mt Binga 2430m
Beira

Bulawayo

Orapa
Francistown

BOTSWANA
Bobonong
Beitbridge

Serowe
Limpopo

Kalahari
Mahalapye

Desert
Pietersburg
Inhambane

Walvis Bay (S. Africa)

Gaborone

Tropic of Capricorn
Xai Xai

Lüderitz
Keetmanshoop

Mafikeng
Krugersdorp
Pretoria
Maputo

Johannesburg
Springs
Mbabane

Upington
Potchefstroom
Germiston
SWAZILAND

Orange
Vereeniging

Vaal
Kroonstad
Newcastle
INDIAN OCEAN

Welkom
Ladysmith

ATLANTIC OCEAN

Kimberley

Maseru
Pietermaritzburg

Bloemfontein
LESOTHO
Thabana Ntlenyana 3482m
Durban

SOUTH AFRICA

Drakensberg

Beaufort West
Queenstown

Great Karroo

Paarl
Worcester
East London

Cape Town
Little Karroo
Uitenhage
Port Elizabeth

Mosselbaai

Cape of Good Hope

Namib Desert

Mozambique Channel

miles
0
500

0
500
kilometres

MOZAMBIQUE
Area: 801,590 sq km (309,496 sq miles)
Population: 17,299,000
Capital: Maputo (pop 2,867,000)

COMOROS
Area: 2,171 sq km (838 sq miles)
Population: 544,000
Capital: Moroni (pop 44,000)

ZIMBABWE
Area: 390,580 sq km (150,804 sq miles)
Population: 11,904,000
Capital: Harare (pop 1,686,000)

SOUTH AFRICA
Area: 1,221,037 sq km (471,445 sq miles)
Population: 42,106,000
Capital: Pretoria (administrative, 692,000), Cape Town (legislative, 1,118,000), Bloemfontein (judicial, 103,000)
Other large cities: Johannesburg (2,027,000) Durban (1,993,000)
Religions: Christianity (78.1%), Hinduism (2.1%), Islam (1.4%), other (18.4%)
Official languages: Afrikaans, English
Currency: Rand

BOTSWANA
Area: 581,730 sq km (224,607 sq miles)
Population: 1,588,000
Capital: Gaborone (pop 193,000)

MADAGASCAR
Area: 587,041 sq km (226,658 sq miles)
Population: 15,051,000
Capital: Antananarivo (pop 1,432,000)

SWAZILAND
Area: 17,363 sq km (6,704 sq miles)
Population: 1,019,000
Capital: Mbabane (pop 73,000)

LESOTHO
Area: 30,355 sq km (11,720 sq miles)
Population: 2,105,000
Capital: Maseru (pop 373,000)

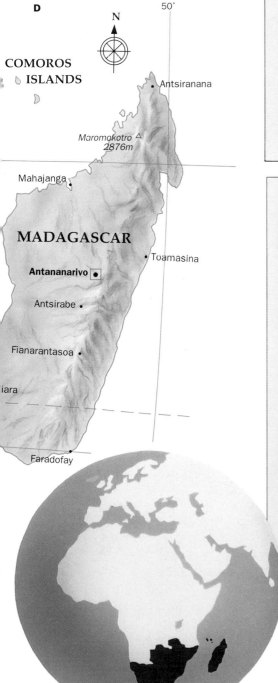

D

N

50°

COMOROS ISLANDS

Antsiranana

Maromokotro △ 2876m

Mahajanga

MADAGASCAR

Antananarivo

Toamasina

Antsirabe

Fianarantsoa

iara

Faradofay

Australia and Oceania

Australia is the only country which is also a continent. It is the smallest of the world's seven continents. Australia is part of a region called Oceania, which also includes New Zealand, Papua New Guinea and many islands of the Pacific Ocean.

The longest river in Australia is the Murray. It flows throughout the year, unlike the slightly longer Darling River, parts of which dry up in winter. Papua New Guinea has the highest mountains in Oceania. New Zealand's highest peak is Mount Cook. Australia's is Mount Kosciusko.

Australia is a mainly dry continent, with only about 19 million people. Most Australians live in a few cities on the coast, including Sydney and Melbourne. The rest of Oceania has about 11 million people.

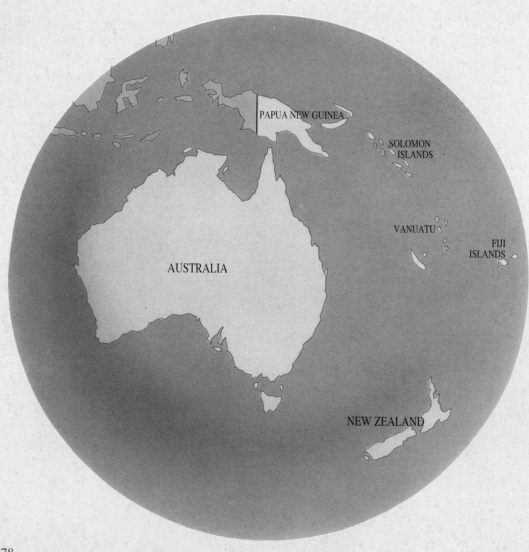

Australia, New Zealand and the Pacific Islands

130°   C   140°   D   150°

1

New Irelan
Wewak   *Bismarck Sea*
Sepik   Rabaul
Madang   *New Britai*
Mt Wilhelm
4508m △   *Boug*
PAPUA NEW GUINEA
Lae   *Solomon*

Arafura Sea   Torres Strait
Port Moresby ▣   *Owen Stanley Range*

Cape York   *Coral Sea*
Melville I.   *Cape
York
Peninsula*

B   *Timor Sea*   Darwin   *Arnhem
Land*   *Gulf of
Carpentaria*   Cooktown
Cairns   *Great*

A   INDIAN
OCEAN   Wyndham   *Barrier*
*Kimberley
Plateau*   **NORTHERN TERRITORY**   Townsville   *Reef*
2   Derby   Tennant Creek
Broome   Richmond   *Dividing*
Mount Isa   Mackay

**Great Sandy
Desert**   *Great*   Rockhampton
20°   Dampier   Port Hedland   **A U S**   **T R A L I A**   **QUEENSLAND**
Macdonnell Range   **Great
Artesian
Basin**   *Range*   *Bund*
Alice Springs   *Marybo*
Gibson Desert   Ayers Rock
△ 867m   **Simpson
Desert**
Musgrave Range
Carnarvon   **WESTERN AUSTRALIA**   Toowoomba   **Bri**
3   *Lake
Eyre*   Ipswich
Mount Magnet   **Great Victoria**   **Desert**   **SOUTH
AUSTRALIA**   *Lis*
Geraldton   *Darling*   *Gra*
Bourke   *Range*
*Lake
Torrens*   Broken Hill   **NEW SOUTH WALES**   Maitland   **Dividing**
Lake
Gairdner   Woomera   **Newcastl**
Kalgoorlie   **Nullarbor**   **Plain**   Port Augusta   **Sydney**
30°   Norseman   Whyalla   Port Pirie   Wagga Wagga   **Wollongong**
Perth   Elizabeth   Canberra
Fremantle   *Great Australian Bight*   **Adelaide**   *Murray*   AUSTRALIAN CAPITAL TERRI
Bunbury   **VICTORIA**   Albury   △Mt Kosciusko
2230m
Kangaroo I.   Bendigo   *Great*
Albany   Ballarat   **Melbourne**
4   **Geelong**

Bass Strait   **Flinders I.**
King I.
40°   **TASMANIA**   Launceston
△Mt Ossa 1617m
5   **Hobart**

miles
0   500
0   500
kilometres

80

Honiara

SOLOMON ISLANDS

Guadalcanal I.

160°

170°

F

N

VANUATU

Vila

NEW CALEDONIA (Fr.)

Nouméa

opic of Capricorn

PACIFIC OCEAN

Norfolk I.

G

Howe I.

Tasman Sea

North Island

Whangarei

Auckland

Hamilton

Lake Taupo

Gisborne

Mt Ruapehu 2797m

Palmerston North

Hastings

Nelson

NEW ZEALAND

South Island

Mt Cook (Aoraki) 3764m

Wellington

Cook Strait

Southern Alps

Christchurch

Timaru

Invercargill

Dunedin

Stewart I.

PAPUA NEW GUINEA
Area: 461,691 sq km (178,260 sq miles)
Highest point: Mount Wilhelm 4,508m (14,790ft)
Population: 4,706,000
Capital and largest city: Port Moresby (pop 152,000)

SOLOMON ISLANDS
Area: 28,446 sq km (10,983 sq miles)
Population: 429,000
Capital and largest city: Honiara (pop 30,000)

NEW ZEALAND
Area: 268,676 sq km (103,736 sq miles)
Population: 3,811,000
Capital: Wellington (pop 326,000)
Other large cities: Auckland (953,000), Christchurch (303,000)
Official language: English
Religion: Christianity
Economy: *Agriculture:* wool, meat, dairy products; *Mining:* natural gas, iron ore, coal; *Industry:* processed foods, wood and paper, textiles, machinery
Currency: New Zealand Dollar
Government: Constitutional monarchy

VANUATU
Area: 14,763 sq km (5,700 sq miles)
Population: 193,000
Capital: Vila (pop 19,000)

AUSTRALIA
Area: 7,686,848 sq km (2,967,909 sq miles)
Highest point: Mt. Kosciusko 2,230m (7,316ft)
Population: 18,967,000
Capital: Canberra (pop 297,000)
Other large cities: Sydney (3,596,000), Melbourne (3,002,000), Brisbane (1,240,000)
Official language: English
Religion: Christianity
Economy: *Agriculture:* wool, meat, wheat, fruit, sugar; *Mining:* bauxite, coal, iron ore, copper, oil and natural gas, uranium; *Industry:* machinery and transport equipment, processed foods, chemicals, iron and steel, paper, textiles
Currency: Australian Dollar
Government: Constitutional monarchy

NEW CALEDONIA (FRANCE)
Area: 19,058 sq km (7,358 sq miles)
Population: 209,000
Capital: Nouméa (pop 65,000)

Pacific Ocean

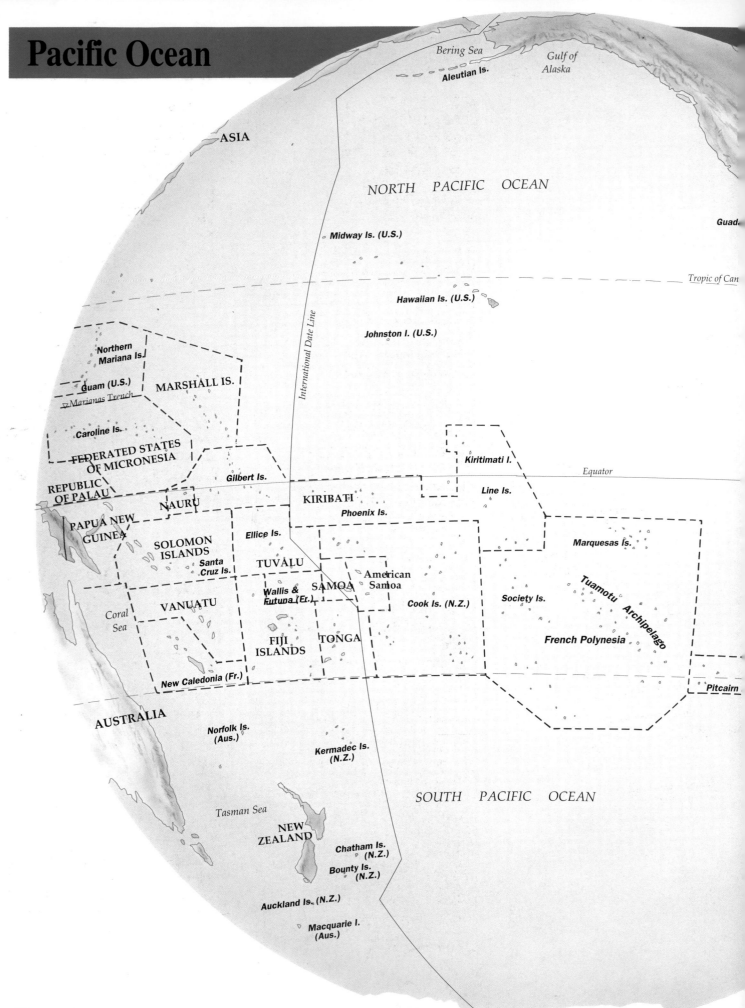

Bering Sea

Gulf of Alaska

Aleutian Is.

ASIA

NORTH   PACIFIC   OCEAN

Guad.

Midway Is. (U.S.)

Tropic of Can

Hawaiian Is. (U.S.)

Johnston I. (U.S.)

Northern Mariana Is.

MARSHALL IS.

International Date Line

Guam (U.S.)

Marianas Trench

Caroline Is.

Kiritimati I.

FEDERATED STATES OF MICRONESIA

Equator

REPUBLIC OF PALAU

Gilbert Is.

KIRIBATI

Line Is.

NAURU

Phoenix Is.

PAPUA NEW GUINEA

Marquesas Is.

SOLOMON ISLANDS

Ellice Is.

SANTA Cruz Is.

TUVALU

American Samoa

Society Is.

Tuamotu Archipelago

Wallis & Futuna (Fr.)

SAMOA

Coral Sea

VANUATU

Cook Is. (N.Z.)

French Polynesia

FIJI ISLANDS

TONGA

New Caledonia (Fr.)

Pitcairn

AUSTRALIA

Norfolk Is. (Aus.)

Kermadec Is. (N.Z.)

SOUTH   PACIFIC   OCEAN

Tasman Sea

NEW ZEALAND

Chatham Is. (N.Z.)

Bounty Is. (N.Z.)

Auckland Is. (N.Z.)

Macquarie I. (Aus.)

PACIFIC OCEAN

Area: 181,000,000 sq km
(69,884,500 sq miles)

Deepest point:
11,033m (33,198ft)
in the Marianas Trench

REPUBLIC OF PALAU

Area: 488 sq km (188 sq miles)

Population: 19,000

Capital: Koror (pop 13,000)

FEDERATED STATES OF MICRONESIA

Area: 702 sq km (271 sq miles)

Population: 116,000

Capital: Palikiv

MARSHALL ISLANDS

Area: 181 sq km (70 sq miles)

Population: 51,000

Capital: Majuro (pop 33,000)

NAURU

Area: 21 sq km (8 sq miles)

Population: 10,000

Capital: Yaren

KIRIBATI

Area: 728 sq km (281 sq miles)

Population: 88,000

Capital: Bairiki (on Tarawa)

International Date Line

The international date line runs
north-south through the central
Pacific Ocean. When crossing the
line from east to west, travellers
lose one day. When crossing from
west to east, they gain a day.

This is because there is a 24-hour
difference between the time on
either side of the line. The line does
not follow longitude 180 degrees
exactly. It bends around islands to
avoid confusion.

TUVALU

Area: 25 sq km (10 sq miles)

Population: 11,000

Capital: Fongafale (on Funafuti atoll)

SAMOA

Area: 2,842 sq km (1,097 sq miles)

Population: 169,000

Capital: Apia (pop 38,000)

FIJI ISLANDS

Area: 18,274 sq km (7,056 sq
miles)

Population: 801,000

Capital: Suva (pop 196,000)

TONGA

Area: 699 sq km (270 sq miles)

Population: 100,000

Capital: Nuku'alofa (pop 37,000)

Atlantic Ocean

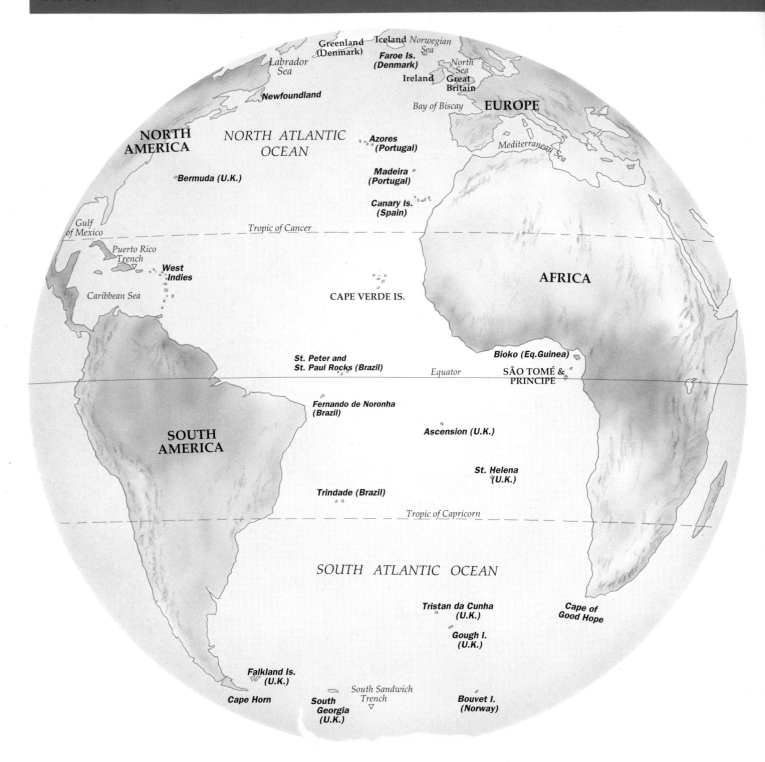

Greenland (Denmark)

Iceland

Norwegian Sea

Labrador Sea

Faroe Is. (Denmark)

North Sea

Ireland Great Britain

Newfoundland

Bay of Biscay EUROPE

NORTH AMERICA

NORTH ATLANTIC OCEAN

Azores (Portugal)

Mediterranean Sea

Bermuda (U.K.)

Madeira (Portugal)

Canary Is. (Spain)

Gulf of Mexico

Tropic of Cancer

Puerto Rico Trench ▽

West Indies

AFRICA

Caribbean Sea

CAPE VERDE IS.

St. Peter and St. Paul Rocks (Brazil)

Bioko (Eq.Guinea)

Equator SÃO TOMÉ & PRINCIPE

Fernando de Noronha (Brazil)

Ascension (U.K.)

SOUTH AMERICA

St. Helena (U.K.)

Trindade (Brazil)

Tropic of Capricorn

SOUTH ATLANTIC OCEAN

Tristan da Cunha (U.K.)

Cape of Good Hope

Gough I. (U.K.)

Falkland Is. (U.K.)

South Sandwich Trench ▽

Cape Horn South Georgia (U.K.)

Bouvet I. (Norway)

ATLANTIC OCEAN
Area: 81,500,000 sq km
(31,467,330 sq miles)
Deepest point: 9,220m (30,250ft)
in the Puerto Rico Trench

INDIAN OCEAN
Area: 74,000,000 sq km
(28,571,560 sq miles)
Deepest point: 7,450m (24,442ft)
in the Java Trench

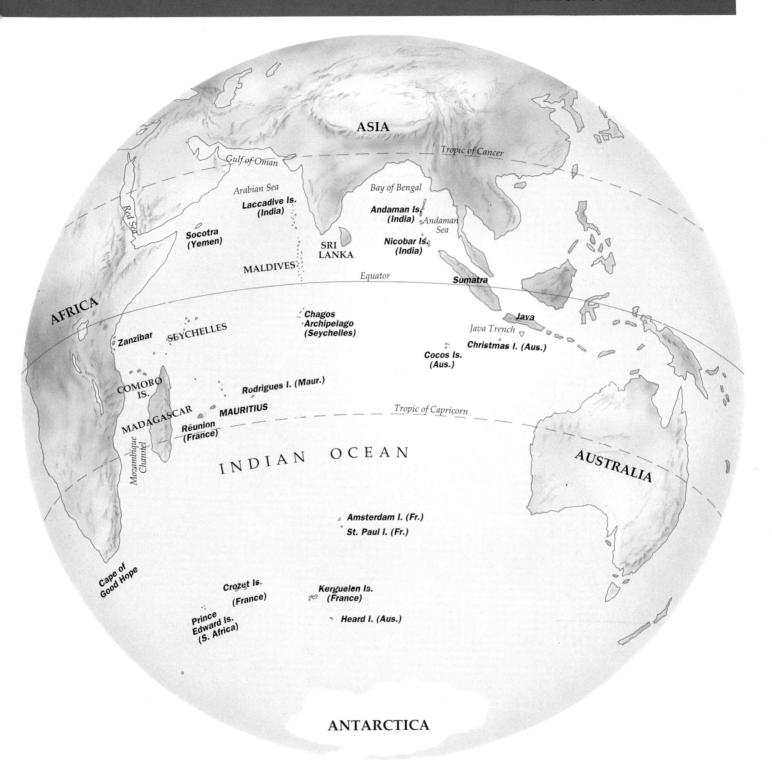

ASIA

Tropic of Cancer

Gulf of Oman

Arabian Sea

Bay of Bengal

**Laccadive Is.
(India)**

Red Sea

**Andaman Is
(India)** *Andaman
Sea*

**Socotra
(Yemen)**

**SRI
LANKA**

**Nicobar Is.
(India)**

MALDIVES

Equator

Sumatra

Java

AFRICA

**Chagos
Archipelago
(Seychelles)**

Java Trench ▽

Zanzibar **SEYCHELLES**

Christmas I. (Aus.)

**Cocos Is.
(Aus.)**

**COMORO
IS.**

Rodrigues I. (Maur.)

Tropic of Capricorn

AUSTRALIA

MADAGASCAR **MAURITIUS**

**Réunion
(France)**

*Mozambique
Channel*

INDIAN OCEAN

Amsterdam I. (Fr.)

St. Paul I. (Fr.)

**Cape of
Good Hope**

**Crozet Is.
(France)**

**Kerguelen Is.
(France)**

**Prince
Edward Is.
(S. Africa)**

Heard I. (Aus.)

ANTARCTICA

MALDIVES
Area: 298 sq km (115 sq miles)
Population: 269,000
Capital: Male (pop 72,000)

SEYCHELLES
Area: 404 sq km (156 sq miles)
Population: 80,000
Capital: Victoria (pop 28,000)

MAURITIUS
Area: 1,865 sq km (720 sq miles)
Population: 1,174,000
Capital: Port Louis (pop 172,000)

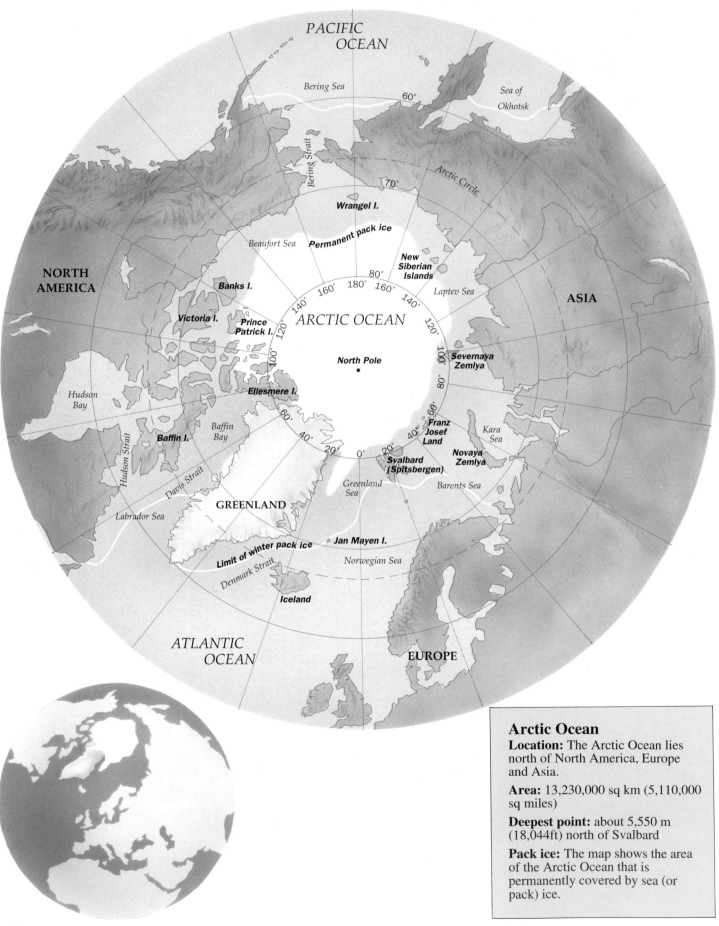

PACIFIC OCEAN

Bering Sea

60°

Sea of Okhotsk

Arctic Circle

70°

Wrangel I.

Beaufort Sea

Permanent pack ice

New Siberian Islands

Laptev Sea

NORTH AMERICA

Banks I.

80°

160° 180° 160°

140°

120°

ARCTIC OCEAN

ASIA

Victoria I.

Prince Patrick I.

North Pole

Severnaya Zemlya

100°

80°

Hudson Bay

Ellesmere I.

60°

Franz Josef Land

Kara Sea

40°

Baffin Bay

20°

Novaya Zemlya

Hudson Strait

Baffin I.

0°

20°

Svalbard (Spitsbergen)

Davis Strait

Greenland Sea

Barents Sea

Labrador Sea

GREENLAND

Jan Mayen I.

Limit of winter pack ice

Norwegian Sea

Denmark Strait

Iceland

ATLANTIC OCEAN

EUROPE

Arctic Ocean

Location: The Arctic Ocean lies north of North America, Europe and Asia.

Area: 13,230,000 sq km (5,110,000 sq miles)

Deepest point: about 5,550 m (18,044ft) north of Svalbard

Pack ice: The map shows the area of the Arctic Ocean that is permanently covered by sea (or pack) ice.

Antarctica

Location: Antarctica is a frozen continent at the South Pole. The waters around Antarctica are sometimes called the Southern Ocean, but many geographers still consider these waters to be part of the Pacific, Atlantic and Indian oceans.

Area: About 14,000,000 sq km (about 5,405,000 sq miles)

Population: None permanent

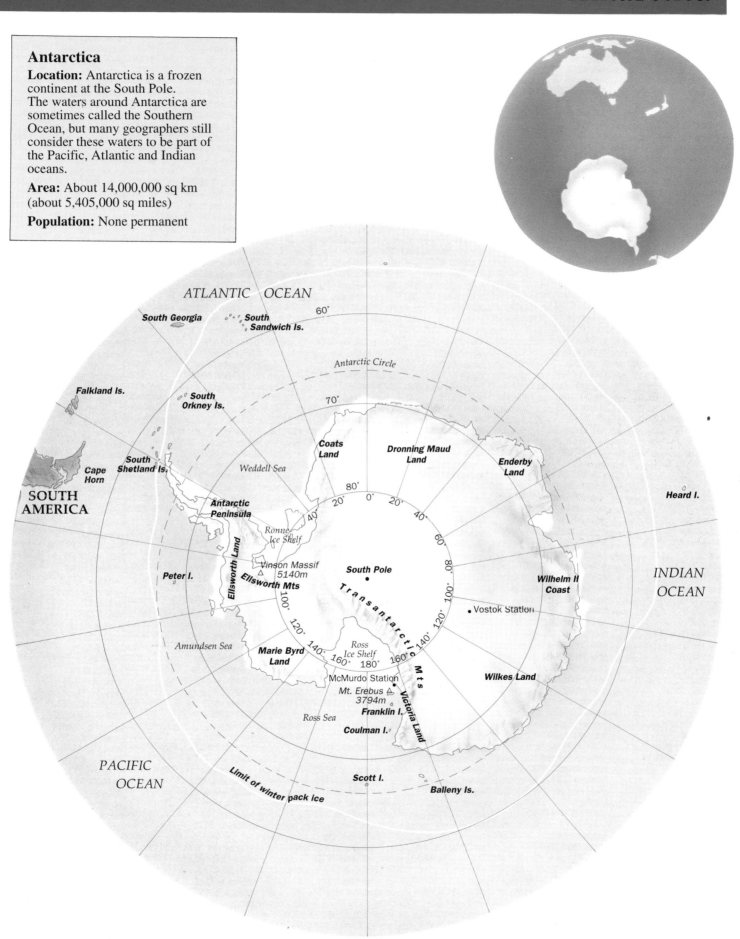

ATLANTIC OCEAN

South Georgia

South Sandwich Is.

Antarctic Circle

60°

Falkland Is.

South Orkney Is.

70°

Coats Land

Dronning Maud Land

Enderby Land

Cape Horn

South Shetland Is.

Weddell Sea

80°

Heard I.

SOUTH AMERICA

Antarctic Peninsula

Ronne Ice Shelf

20° 0° 20° 40°

60°

Peter I.

Ellsworth Land

Vinson Massif 5140m

Ellsworth Mts

South Pole

Wilhelm II Coast

INDIAN OCEAN

80° 80°

100°

100°

Vostok Station

Transantarctic

120°

120°

Amundsen Sea

Marie Byrd Land

140°

Ross Ice Shelf

160° 180° 160°

Wilkes Land

M t s

Victoria Land

McMurdo Station

Mt. Erebus 3794m

Franklin I.

Ross Sea

Coulman I.

PACIFIC OCEAN

Limit of winter pack ice

Scott I.

Balleny Is.

St. Petersburg (Fa.) 25 F3
St. Petersburg (Russia) 54 A2
St. Pierre & Miquelon 19 E3
St. Pölten 50 D2
St-Quentin 42 E2
St. Tropez 43 G5
St. Vincent & The Grenadines 33 E4
Sakai 65 F2
Sakakawea L. 26 A1
Sakhalin I. 55 G2
Sala y Gómez 83
Sal I. 72 B1
Salalah 61 D5
Salamanca 46 C2
Salekhard 54 C1
Salem (India) 63 D6
Salem (Ore.) 28 C2
Salerno 52 C3
Salina 26 B3
Salisbury (Md.) 23 F4
Salisbury (U.K.) 45 F5
Salta 37 C5
Saltillo 30 D2
Salt Lake City 29 E2
Salto 37 D6
Salton Sea 29 D4
Salvador 36 F4
Salween R. 64 C3
Salzburg 50 C3
Salzgitter 50 C1
Samar 67 D2
Samara 54 B2
Samarinda 67 C4
Samarqand 54 C3
Samoa 82
Samos 53 F4
Samothraki 53 E3
Sam Rayburn Res. 24 D2
Samsun 59 D1
San R. 51 F2
Sana 60 B5
San Ambrosio I. 37 B5
San Angelo 24 B2
San Antonio 24 C3
San Bernardino 28 D4
San Carlos 67 D2
Sancti Spiritus 32 B2
San Cristóbal 36 B2
San Diego 28 D4
Sandviken 48 G4
San Félix I. 37 A5
San Fernando 46 B4
San Francisco 28 C3
Sangihe Is. 67 D3
San Joaquin R. 28 C3
San Jose 28 C3
San José 31 H6
San Juan (Argentina) 37 C6
San Juan (Puerto Rico) 33 D3
Sanlúcar 46 B4
San Luis Potosi 30 D3
San Marino 52 B2
San Miguel 31 G5
San Miguel de Tucumán 37 C5
San Pedro Sula 31 G4
San Salvador 31 G5
San Salvador I. 32 C2
San Sebastián 47 E1
Santa Ana (Calif.) 28 D4
Santa Ana (El Salvador) 31 G5
Santa Antão 72 A1
Santa Barbara 28 D4
Santa Clara 32 B2
Santa Cruz (Bolivia) 36 C4
Santa Cruz (Canary Is.) 46 I5
Santa Cruz Is. 82
Santa Fe (Argentina) 37 C6
Santa Fe (N. Mex.) 29 F3
Santa Maria (Brazil) 37 D5
Santa Maria (Calif.) 28 C4
Santa Marta 36 B1

Santander 46 D1
Santa Rosa 28 C3
Santee R. 25 F2
Santiago (Chile) 37 B6
Santiago (Dominican Republic) 33 C3
Santiago de Compostela 46 A1
Santiago de Cuba 32 B2
Santiago del Estero 37 C5
Santiago Mts. 24 B3
Santo Domingo 33 D3
Santos 37 E5
Sao Francisco R. E4
São Luis 36 E3
Saône R. 43 F3
São Paulo 37 E5
São Tiago I. 72 B1
São Tomé 74 A1
Sao Tomé & Principe 74 A1
Sapele 73 H5
Sapporo 65 F2
Sarajevo 53 D2
Sarasota 25 F3
Saratov 54 B2
Sarawak 67 C3
Sardinia 52 A3
Sargodha 63 C2
Sarh 71 D4
Sark 45 H5
Sarmi 67 E4
Saskatchewan 18 B3
Saskatchewan R. 18 B3
Saskatoon 18 B3
Sassandra R. 72 E5
Sassari 52 A3
Satu Mare 53 E1
Saudi Arabia 60 B4
Sault Ste. Marie (Canada) 19 C3
Sault Ste. Marie (Mich.) 27 E1
Sava R. 52 C2
Savannah 25 F2
Savannah R. 25 F2
Sayan Mts. 55 D2
Scafell Pike 45 E3
Scarborough (Tobago) 33 E4
Scarborough (U.K.) 45 F3
Schaffhausen 43 H3
Schweinfurt 50 C2
Schwerin 50 C1
Scilly, Isles of 45 C6
Scotland 45 D2
Scott I. 87
Scottsbluff 26 A2
Scranton 23 F3
Scunthorpe 45 F4
Scutari L. 53 D2
Seattle 28 C1
Ségou 70 B3
Segovia 46 C2
Seine R. 42 D2
Sekondi-Takoradi 73 F5
Selma 25 E2
Selvas 36 C3
Semarang 67 C4
Semipalatinsk 55 D2
Sendai 65 F2
Senegal 72 D4
Senegal R. 72 D3
Seoul 65 E2
Sepik River 80 D1
Serbia & Montenegro 53 D2
Serowe 76 B2
Serra da Estrela 46 B2
Serra de Alvelos 46 B3
Serrai 53 E3
Serrania de Cuenca 47 E2
Sète 42 E5
Sétif 70 C1
Setúbal 46 A3
Sevastopol 54 A2
Severnaya Zemlya 55 E1
Severn R. 45 E5

Seville 46 C4
Seward 28 B1
Seychelles 85
Seydhisfjordhur 48 C2
Seyhan R. 59 C2
Sfax 70 D1
Shache 64 A2
Shanghai 65 E3
Shannon R. 44 B4
Shantou 65 D3
Shaoguan 65 D3
Shaoyang 64 D3
Sharjah 61 E3
Shebelle R. 71 G4
Sheboygan 27 D2
Sheffield 45 F4
Shenandoah R. 23 E4
Shenyang 65 E2
Sherbro I. 72 D5
Sheridan 29 F2
Sherman 24 C2
Shetland Is. 45 H2
Shijiazhuang 65 D2
Shikoku 65 F2
Shiraz 60 D3
Shire R. 76 C2
Shkodër 53 D2
Sholapur 63 D5
Shreveport 24 D2
Shrewsbury 45 E4
Shumen 53 F2
Shuqra 60 C6
Shushtar 60 C2
Siberut 66 A4
Sibiu 53 E2
Sicily 52 B4
Sidi-bel-Abbès 70 B1
Sidon 59 C3
Siedlce 51 F1
Siena 52 B2
Sierra de Gredos 46 C2
Sierra Leone 72 D5
Sierra Madre del Sur 30 E4
Sierra Madre Occidental 30 C2
Sierra Madre Oriental 30 E3
Sierra Morena 46 C3
Sierra Nevada (Spain) 46 D4
Sierra Nevada (USA) 28 D3
Siglufjördhur 48 B1
Sil R. 46 B1
Silgarhi 63 E3
Silifke 59 C2
Silistra 53 F2
Simeulue 66 A3
Simpson Desert 80 C3
Singapore 66 B3
Sintang 67 C3
Sinuiju 65 E2
Sioux City 26 B2
Sioux Falls 26 B2
Siping 65 E2
Siracusa 52 C4
Siret R. 53 E2
Sisophon 66 B2
Sitka 28 B1
Sivas 59 D2
Skagerrak 48 E5
Skagway 28 B1
Skegness 45 G4
Skellefteå 48 H3
Skellefte R. 48 G3
Skien 48 E4
Skiros 53 E3
Skopje 53 D3
Skye 45 C2
Slagelse 48 E5
Slavonski Brod 53 D2
Sligo 44 B3
Sliven 53 F2
Slovak Republic 51 E2
Slovenia 52 C1

Slupsk 50 D1
Smederevo 53 D2
Smolensk 54 A2
Snake R. 29 D1
Snowdon, Mt. 45 D4
Society Is. 82
Socotra 85
Sofia 53 E2
Sogne Fiord 48 D4
Sokodé 73 G5
Sokoto 73 H4
Sokoto R. 73 G4
Solomon Is. 81 F1
Solomon Sea 80 E1
Solothurn 43 G3
Somali Republic 71 G4
Somerset I. 19 C2
Somesul R. 53 E1
Somme R. 42 E2
Songkhla 66 B3
Sorocaba 37 E5
Soria 47 D2
Sousse 70 D1
South Africa 76 B3
Southampton 45 F5
Southampton I. 19 C2
South Australia 80 C3
South Bend 27 D2
South Carolina 25 F2
South China Sea 67 C2
South Dakota 26 A1
South Downs 45 F5
Southend-on-Sea 45 G5
Southern Alps 81 F5
Southern Uplands 45 D3
South Georgia 84
South I. 81 F5
South Korea 65 E2
South Orkney Is. 87
South Pole 87
Southport 45 E4
South Sandwich Is. 87
South Sandwich Trench 84
South Shetland Is. 87
South Shields 45 F3
South Uist 44 C2
Spain 46 C3
Spanish Town 32 B3
Sparks 28 D3
Spartanburg 25 F2
Spencer 26 B2
Spey R. 45 E2
Split 52 C2
Spokane 29 D1
Springfield (Ill.) 27 D3
Springfield (Mass.) 23 G3
Springfield (Mo.) 26 C3
Springfield (O.) 27 E3
Springfield (Vt.) 23 H2
Springs 76 B3
Sri Lanka 63 E7
Srinagar 63 C2
Stafford 45 E4
Stamford 23 G3
Stanley 37 D8
Stanovoy Range 55 F2
Stara Zagora 53 E2
State College 23 E3
Stavanger 48 D4
Steinkjer 48 E3
Sterling 29 G2
Steubenville 27 E2
Stewart I. 81 F5
Steyr 50 D2
Stockholm 48 G4
Stockport 45 E4
Stockton (Calif.) 28 C3
Stockton (England) 45 F3
Stoke-on-Trent 45 E4
Stornoway 45 C1
Stralsund 50 C1

Stranraer 45 D3
Strasbourg 43 G2
Struma R. 53 E3
Stuttgart 50 B2
Subotica 53 D1
Sucre 36 C4
Sudan 71 E3
Sudbury 19 C3
Sudeten Mts. 50 D2
Suez 71 F2
Suez Canal 71 F1
Sukabumi 66 B4
Sukkur 62 B3
Sula Is. 67 D4
Sulaiman Range 62 B3
Sulawesi 67 D4
Sulu Sea 67 C3
Sumatra 66 B3
Sumba 67 C4
Sumbawa 67 C4
Sumter 25 F2
Sunbury 23 F3
Sunderland 45 F3
Sundsvall 48 G3
Superior 26 C1
Superior, L. 19 C3
Surabaya 67 C4
Surakarta 67 C4
Surat 63 C4
Surgut 54 C1
Surinam 36 D2
Suzhou 65 E3
Svalbard (Spitsbergen) 86
Sverdlovsk, see Yekaterinburg
Swansea 45 E5
Swaziland 76 C3
Sweden 48 F4
Swindon 45 F5
Switzerland 43 G3
Sydney (Australia) 80 E4
Sydney (Canada) 19 D3
Syracuse 23 F2
Syr Darya R. 54 C2
Syria 59 D3
Syrian Desert 59 D3
Szczecin 50 D1
Szeged 51 E3
Székesfehérvar 50 E3
Szombathely 50 D3

T
Tabora 75 C2
Tabriz 60 C1
Tabuk 60 A3
Tacna 36 B4
Tacoma 28 C1
Taegu 65 E2
Taejon 65 E2
Tahat, Mt. 70 C2
Tahoe L. 28 D3
Taichung 65 E3
Tainan 65 E3
Taipei 65 E3
Taiwan 65 E3
Taiyuan 65 D2
Taiz 60 B6
Tajikistan 54 C3
Tajo (Tagus) R. 46 C3
Taklimakan Desert 64 A2
Talaud Is. 67 D3
Talavera 46 C3
Talca 37 B6
Talcahuano 37 B6
Tallahassee 25 F2
Tallinn 54 A2
Tambov 54 B2
Tampa 25 F3
Tampere 48 H4
Tampico 30 E3

Tana L. 71 F3
Tana R. 75 D2
Tandil 37 D6
Tanga 75 D2
Tanganyika L. 75 C2
Tangier 70 B1
Tangshan 65 D2
Tanimbar Is. 67 E4
Tanjungkarang 66 B4
Tanzania 75 C2
Tapachula 31 F5
Tapajós R. 36 D3
Taranto 52 C3
Tarbes 42 D5
Tarkwa 73 F5
Tarragona 47 F2
Tarsus 59 C2
Tashkent (see Toshkent)
Tasmania 80 D5
Tasman Sea 81 F4
Taunton 45 E5
Taupo L. 81 G4
Taurus Mts. 59 C2
Tawau 67 C3
Tay R. 45 E2
Tbilisi 54 B2
Tegucigalpa 31 G5
Tehran 60 D1
Teide, Pico de 46 I5
Tekirdag 58 A1
Tel Aviv-Yafo 59 C3
Temuco 37 B6
Tenby 45 D5
Tenerife 46 I5
Tennant Creek 80 C2
Tennessee 25 E1
Tennessee R. 25 E2
Tepic 30 D3
Teresina 36 E3
Terni 52 B2
Terre Haute 27 D3
Tete 76 C2
Tétouan 70 B1
Texarkana 24 D2
Texas 24 C2
Texoma L. 24 C2
Thabana Ntlenyana 76 B3
Thailand 66 B2
Thailand, Gulf of 66 B2
Thames R. 45 F5
Thar Desert 62 C3
Thasos 53 E2
Thessaloniki 53 E3
Thief River Falls 26 B1
Thiès 72 C4
Thika 75 D2
Thimphu 63 F3
Thionville 43 G2
Thira 53 E4
Thule 19 D2
Thun 43 G3
Thunder Bay 19 C3
Thuringian Forest 50 C2
Thurso 45 E1
Tianjin 65 D2
Tian Shan 64 A2
Tiber R. 52 B2
Tiberias L. 59 C3
Tibesti Mts. 71 D2
Tibetan Plateau 64 B2
Ticino R. 52 A2
Tierra del Fuego 37 C8
Tigris R. 60 B2
Tijuana 30 A1
Timaru 81 G5
Timbuktu 70 B3
Timişoara 53 D2
Timmins 19 C3
Timor 67 D4
Timor Sea 80 B2
Tinos 53 E4

95